Fluorescent Light Gardening

Elaine C. Cherry

D. VAN NOSTRAND COMPANY, INC.
PRINCETON, NEW JERSEY
toronto   new york   london

D. VAN NOSTRAND COMPANY, INC.
120 Alexander St., Princeton, New Jersey (*Principal office*)
24 West 40 Street, New York 18, New York

D. VAN NOSTRAND COMPANY, LTD.
358, Kensington High Street, London, W.14, England

D. VAN NOSTRAND COMPANY (Canada), LTD.
25 Hollinger Road, Toronto 16, Canada

Library of Congress Catalog Card No. 65-18462

PRINTED IN THE UNITED STATES OF AMERICA

For HCM

PREFACE

There's light enough for wot I've got to do.

CHARLES DICKENS

LIVING, GROWING, FLOWERING PLANTS
make home a happier place, whether home is a cottage or estate in the
country, a penthouse or one-room flat in the city, a comfortable place in
the suburbs, or a home on wheels. Electricity and a green-souled inhabi-
tant—that is all it takes to make indoor gardens without sunlight.

The use of light other than sunlight to aid plant growth sometimes
is called *phytoillumination.** I have successfully used light other than sunlight to grow many kinds of plants in my home, but I hardly ever say that
I practice phytoillumination. I call it "fluorescent light gardening."

Of the many kinds of artificial light available—tungsten, neon, mercury
vapor, carbon arc, whale oil and kerosene lamps, and even tallow candles
—fluorescent light possesses the greatest number of desirable characteristics
for growing plants. Fluorescent light more nearly duplicates the colors of
the solar spectrum than any other kind of artificial light; it is cool to
handle, furnishing the plants with abundant light without much damaging heat; and its light spreads easily. Above all, fluorescent light sources
are economical in terms of the amount of light emitted for the power
that is consumed.

In our home, we use fluorescent lamps in the cool greenhouse to force
tulips, hyacinths and other hardy and semihardy bulbs into bloom exactly
when we want them; to display plants attractively on the greenhouse
side of the living-room picture window; and generally to supplement the
bleak light of winter's short and often dull days.

Indoor aquariums are flooded with fluorescent light, both to display
the tropical creatures and the aquatic plants and to supply light for plant

---

* *Phyto*, meaning *a plant* or *plants*, comes from the Greek word *phyton*. The
term "phytoillumination" first appeared in August, 1961, in a bulletin written
by Carl J. Bernier of Sylvania Lighting Products, and Stuart Dunn of the University of New Hampshire (Bulletin 0-230, issued by the Commercial Engineering
Department of Sylvania Electric Products).

and fish life. Shadow boxes, inset in a living-room wall, are fitted with circline fluorescent fixtures and lamps and the prettiest available plants are exhibited in the niches. We use fluorescent lights over terrariums, and over electric propagating cases where seeds are germinated and cuttings are rooted for both indoor and outdoor gardens.

We have several small indoor gardens, fluorescent lighted, scattered about our house, mostly in places that the builder never intended to hold gardens: the fireplace, the spice cabinets in the kitchen, the bookshelves in my study.

And I have my "plant factory"—two rooms devoted entirely to fluorescent light culture. Here, without a single ray of sunlight, grows a vast array of flowering plants: cacti and succulents, tender Dutch bulbs, tropical plants from rhizomes and tubers, geraniums, annuals, orchids, and the two plant families dearest to me, begonias and gesneriads.

I do not know exactly why I am so enamored of begonias. It may be because the Begonia Lady, Bernice Brilmayer, was my dear friend. Nor is it clear why I am so favorably disposed toward the gesneriads (gloxinias, episcias, columneas, achimenes, streptocarpus, and the other "kissing cousins" of the African violet). I am devoted to the special people who have taught me so much about them: Elvin McDonald, Betty Prescott, Bruce Thompson, Paul Arnold, Harold Moore, Robert Lee, and others. Begonias and gesneriads are ideal subjects for artificial light gardening, and both families offer a marvelous variety of form and color in jewel-like leaves and gorgeous blossoms. Both plant families provide flowers indoors during the winter months when plant life and color are so scarce and so appreciated.

In my plant factory grow unrelated but fascinating plants such as cotton, coffee, tea, Norfolk Island pine, vining plants that climb around the uprights, and trailing plants that cascade from the edges of the benches. The so-called green foliage plants, which do not really need much light to exist, provide some of the most delightful (also some of the most frustrating) experiences when fluorescent light culture encourages them to produce their strange flowers.

I grow plants indoors for the pleasure of their company, and for that reason only. I experiment, of course, all the time. But not with growth chambers under a scientist's ideal conditions, where all of the factors of environment can be controlled perfectly and consistently. I grow ornamental plants which sooner or later will flower when I provide the right environmental factors for plant growth indoors. In our home, the general conditions are probably much like yours.

We amateur gardeners really cannot use very much of the information available from scientific studies of plant growth under controlled conditions. We raise our plants in homes where people and pets live, where doors are opened and closed a hundred times a day, where the maximum temperature usually cannot be controlled in the summertime and the minimum temperature in some instances cannot be controlled during the winter, where the atmosphere is almost always drier than plants like, where ventilation depends on an open window, where people go in and out all day long without knowing or caring that they may have carried insects about on their clothing, where facilities such as water and storage space are located for the convenience of people and not of plants, where dust settles on green leaves that will never feel the healing touch of gentle rain, and where the light that plants need is usually available only at a window sill and sometimes not even there.

I have wondered, now and then, if Nature foresaw that people would pull plants from their homes in the ground, transport them to alien territory, confine their roots in a pot, and command them to grow. People all over the world have been doing this for centuries, gladdening their eyes, exciting their noses, and sweetening their souls. But plants are dependent upon the operation of natural laws, and I have learned through experience that my plants will grow to their beautiful best only when I have learned about their needs and their native conditions, and have simulated their natural environment indoors to the best of my ability.

Nature's laws can be bent now and then, but not broken altogether. Certain balances cannot be destroyed without injuring the plants. We can surround a plant with an artificial environment which duplicates or closely approaches that of nature. The artificial environment may even be better suited to plant growth than the natural one because it is more uniform and free from plant enemies. This can be true of fluorescent light gardening in our homes with a minimum of equipment and effort.

Light, however, is only one necessity of plant growth. Plants also need warmth, humidity, air, water, nutrition, growing media, and pest and disease control in order to thrive. All these factors, individually and in combination, influence the health, appearance, and quality of a plant grown indoors under lights. All these cultural needs must be provided in balance, according to a plant's requirements. Variations in the quality and intensity of light may require corresponding adjustment of these other factors if the cultural requirements of the plant are to be fulfilled and the plant is to enjoy its artificial environment.

Some plants are easy to grow under fluorescent lights indoors, others are more demanding and more difficult. I suppose that there *are* plants that will grow only in a greenhouse or conservatory, but I can give you no list of ornamental plants that *cannot* be grown under fluorescent light culture. Except for alpine plants and similar hardy subjects, and the garden biennials that require a year in the open before they flower the second season, I do not know what plants those might be. A plant of suitable size that grows and flowers in natural light will grow and flower in fluorescent light *if* and *when* the gardener finds the right combination of cultural factors: temperature, relative humidity, nutrition; intensity, day length, color of light, etc.

I have tried diligently in the two years prior to writing this book to find the window-sill house plants that would not grow (that is, those that would die) when deprived of all light except that from fluorescent lamps. I worked much harder at it than I might have if I had not received a letter that said, "I'd like to make a suggestion for your book— please tell us what won't grow under lights. I recently purchased some miniature geraniums and was told they won't grow under the lights. It made me wonder what else wouldn't. I would find such a chapter most helpful and hope you can include it."

Well, I grow miniature geraniums under fluorescent lights, and I know many other house-plant growers who do. Geraniums of all sorts require lots of light to produce flowers and they do not mind one bit if that light is natural sunlight or fluorescent light, as long as there is enough of it.

Light alone does not compensate for deficiencies in the other elements of culture for house plants. Turning on a fluorescent light over a potted plant will not work a miracle. The miracle happened when the plant came into being, and from that point on it is up to the gardener to provide the combination of conditions which the plant's nature demands.

It is my affectionate wish that those who engage in gardening-by-computer and plant-culture-by-theory will stop trying to conquer nature by mental effort alone, soil their hands in the life-giving earth, and try to grow the plants they love as best they can. The pleasure that will be theirs will be immense when they follow nature's lead.

ELAINE C. CHERRY

Merrick, New York
January, 1965

ACKNOWLEDGMENTS

My acknowledgments of assistance with this book begin with a stranger at an International Flower Show in New York City from whose hand I accepted a membership application blank for the American Gloxinia Society. It was easier to take the piece of paper and move on than to stop and explain that "gloxinia" meant nothing to me and the name sounded like some undesirable nasal condition. Several months later, in a coat pocket I found the crumpled application form and mailed it, prompted more by curiosity than anything else. I recalled that the stranger *had* mentioned that I, too, could grow beautiful plants.

Through *The Gloxinian,* I met its founder and editor, Elvin McDonald; and through him, the late Bernice Brilmayer. I would like to tell you the kind of friends these two people have been to me: the kind I could telephone at any time of the day or night to request advice or to share a fascinating horticultural discovery; the kind who shared plants lovingly and who were forever giving me seeds, seedlings, cuttings, and plants with the admonition to "see what you can do with it under fluorescent lights." Personal and telephonic visits with Bernice terminated with her untimely death, but I still learn from her books. I acquired a great number of the original plants grown by Bernice as she was writing her various books, and I still have many of them or their progeny. Elvin and Bernice between them were responsible for ensnaring me in the garden of indoor ornamental plants in which I now live.

My husband, Norman J. Cherry, is an electrical and mechanical genius. His ability and willingness to assist my indoor gardening with his knowledge of the creation and control of environment made it possible for me to garden successfully with fluorescent light from the beginning, and now to write this book so that others may share our knowledge and experience. Long before we knew that a manufacturer was working on a fluorescent lamp for plant growth, Norman had selected the fluorescent lamps for our indoor gardens according to the relative quantities of red and blue light emitted by the various white fluorescent lamps then available. It was when he finally got around to suggesting to Sylvania Electric Products, Inc., that there might be a market for a plant growth lamp that we learned that Sylvania had such a project in the experimental stage. An instrument engineer and a teacher, Norman obtained or improvised and made the mechanical and electrical contrivances that are so useful in my fluorescent light gardens. He has the happy faculty of being able to explain electrical, mechanical, and natural phenomena in non-scientific language. I am beholden to many for help with this book, but to none more than to Norman Cherry.

I am indebted to the men in the Commercial Engineering Department of Sylvania Electric Products, Inc., especially to Carl J. Bernier and Christos C. Mpelkas, for much practical information and for the privilege of being among the very first to use Gro-Lux lamps in my indoor gardens. Gordon Hurst and A. J. Rugo, of Sylvania's Garden City, New York, office, responded with great friendliness and dispatch to my frequent urgent telephone calls for literature and lamps.

J. A. Dickerhoff, Long Island Lighting Company, Mineola, New York, an accomplished indoor gardener himself, furnished me with electrical publications, catalogs of electrical equipment suppliers, and data on the cost of gardening with fluorescent light.

Gardening friends have given me tips and hints and clues to successful fluorescent light gardening. Notable among these people are Mr. and Mrs. Thomas Powell, New York City, who can bring almost any orchid to flower under fluorescent light and who supplied most of the cultural information on orchids. Gordon Foster, Maplewood, New Jersey, furnished the information about fluorescent light culture of ferns.

A debt I thoroughly enjoy owing is that to my friend Mrs. William F. Prescott, East Islip, Long Island, New York. Betty is my idea of a good gardener. She has a way with African violets, gloxinias, and other gesneriads that is matched by few. But more than this, she is generous with her time, her talents, and her plants. The numerous fluorescent light gardens in her home have always been open to me to look at, talk about, and photograph, and many of the cultural suggestions in this book originated with her.

Michael J. Kartuz, Wilmington, Massachusetts, has given me many plants and much help on their culture under fluorescent light.

To the many authors of horticultural books to which I refer so frequently I owe an incalculable obligation.

My grateful acknowledgments of assistance end where it all began, with the stranger at the Flower Show who introduced me to this wonderful world of indoor gardening. No longer a stranger, Paul Arnold is a grower of and writer about gesneriads and other indoor plants. From his lifetime of experience as a photographic and motion picture engineer, he gave valuable assistance with the section on how to measure light. Author and technical editor, he read this book in manuscript and patiently helped me to say what I mean and mean what I say.

CONTENTS

ILLUSTRATIONS

Drawings and photographs by Norman J. Cherry except where noted

PART ONE

The Mechanics and Equipment of Fluorescent Light Gardening

To me every hour of the light and dark is a miracle,
Every cubic inch of space is a miracle.

WALT WHITMAN

There is no season such delight can bring,
As summer, autumn, winter, and the spring.
WILLIAM SHAKESPEARE

1

Where to Place a Fluorescent Light Garden

A fluorescent light garden can be located almost any place in a home, office, factory, store, school, or other building where three conditions are in force: 1) reconciliation of the eternal contest between the square foot and the round dollar; (2) source of electric power; (3) availability of the elements of proper culture, in addition to light, for the plants you want to grow. Sometimes there is a fourth condition to be reckoned with: will the rest of the family tolerate with good humor the aberration of a mother or dad, husband or wife, who tosses the galoshes and tennis rackets out of the closet under the stairs to install a flower garden? Almost always, the non-green thumbers will come around to your side when they see what you can do with some plants and a few cents worth of electricity in a practically unused space indoors. Before long, they will be "bragging on you" and bringing their friends in for an indoor-garden tour. It is better to make sure the family is with you before you eviscerate the television cabinet to convert it into a fluorescent lighted shadow-box garden!

FIG. 1 Peperomias, impatiens, begonias, and small foliage plants have taken over the spice cabinets in the author's kitchen.

Bear in mind two things. Your fluorescent light garden will require humidity, ventilation, and a reasonable control of temperature day and night. The dimensions of available fluorescent fixtures and lamps are inflexible. A fixture 48 inches long cannot be pretzeled into a 47-inch space or bent around corners.

Survey the areas in your home where you would like to have a garden. From basement to attic, and including these areas, you will find a surprising number of spots for indoor gardens: closets, porches, rooms not needed for living purposes, hallways,

FIG. 2   Narrow shelf near ceiling holds tiny pots of miniature cacti irradiated by a 40-watt lamp. Planter with two 20-watt lamps holds assortment of begonias, coleus, fancy-leaved geraniums. Author's kitchen. *Planter from Plant Growth Supplies.*

dormers and ells, bathrooms, kitchens, laundry rooms, pantries, garages; doorways or passages between rooms, cabinets, cupboards, bookcases, fireplaces, room dividers, counters under shelves and cabinets, corners of rooms, wide ledges under windows. Every home and apartment has at least one odd, heretofore useless nook that can be made alive and charming with a beautiful indoor garden spotlighted dramatically by a fluorescent lighting fixture.

FIG. 3 Geraniums and a miniature dahlia grow in a fluorescent lighted planter atop the washer-dryer. Sunlight has never touched the plants in the author's kitchen—it is an inside, windowless room.

FIG. 4   A long narrow hall on second floor is lined with fluorescent light gardens of African violets. Home of Mrs. William F. Prescott.

I have heard of fluorescent light gardens in the most unlikely locations: that most dismal of places, a coalbin, cleaned and whitewashed; a bomb shelter; a basement room used in "the good old days" to store the summer's canning and preserving efforts. One gentleman I know must go down to the basement and then up a ladder to get to his fluorescent light gardens— he has one in each of the crawl spaces under the first floor of his house. Admittedly, the crawl spaces are higher than most, the gentleman is exceedingly thin, and the ventilation and humidity are excellent. Each 12-inch-wide space has a 2-tube

FIG. 5 Fluorescent light gardens in a basement. Home of Mrs. William F. Prescott.

strip fixture 48 inches long and 4 inches wide, suspended from the ceiling of the crawl space. The trays of plants slide in and out like file drawers, and the gardener gets around to each on a traveling ladder he bought second-hand from a library that was revising its equipment.

Some areas in the home, such as bookcases, closets, or shadow boxes, at first glance may seem ideal for a garden but prove unsatisfactory in use because they are difficult to ventilate, or the required humidity cannot be maintained without damaging wallpaper, furniture, or furnishings. In most homes the horticulturally unsatisfactory areas are usually in the living room, where appearance is important. Nevertheless, growing plants can be used decoratively, displayed at their prime under fluorescent light and later returned to a more suitable growing area to be reconditioned for another display.

The basement is the most popular place for fluorescent light gardens in homes in most parts of the United States and Canada. Usually it is the one part of the house where space is available. More important, a basement is well suited to fluorescent light culture because it provides several of the environmental conditions needed by plants: stable air—very few doors opening and closing to create drafts; temperature 60 to 70 degrees F. summer and winter; usually cooler at night in winter; water is usually handy and splashes and drips do not hurt the floor; the mess of handling soil and potting plants is out of the way of family and furnishings.

The seldom-used bedroom or guest room is probably the next most popular indoor-garden site. After that comes the enclosed heated porch.

An attic is usually the least popular place for a fluorescent light garden—inconvenient, and often too cold in winter and too hot in summer.

My first fluorescent light garden (on the first floor because we have no basement) was made of "we don't need it but don't throw it out" gems from the attic. An old drop-leaf table was rigged with an industrial fluorescent light fixture propped at each corner on bricks and swathed in a dry cleaner's plastic bag. This pioneer indoor garden of mine held four gloxinias, four tuberous begonias and two African violets, and they all soon smothered under their unventilated, superheated shroud.

This first garden was set up, temporarily I thought, in a corner of one of two adjoining rooms (former living and dining rooms) which we intended to convert into a sewing room and

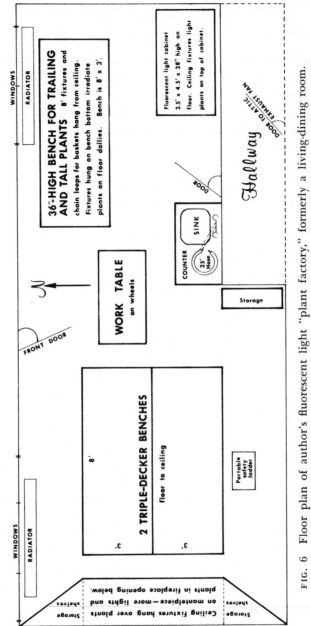

FIG. 6 Floor plan of author's fluorescent light "plant factory," formerly a living-dining room.

a den. We had not foregone living and dining, but had built a large indoor-outdoor living room as an addition to the house.

My husband, an electrical engineer with special experience in the design and application of instruments for the automatic control of temperature, humidity, and other environmental factors, was skeptical but willing to assist in my project for indoor gardening under fluorescent light. Then, and now, to him a house plant was either a geranium or an iron-cross begonia (*Begonia masoniana*). These are the only house plants he admits to recognizing, but he is a champion grower of tomatoes outdoors. Whenever I acquired a new plant, learned its history and habitat, and decided that it would probably *live* under any of several indoor conditions but would do *best* with one specific combination of humidity, temperature, and light, Norman answered these challenges by rigging areas in our home that provided the prescribed conditions.

Within two months, the converted living-dining rooms were a hodgepodge of unmatched fluorescent light fixtures swung over tables, benches, and reclaimed cabinets—anything on which plants could sit and over which lights could be hung, including the mantelpiece of the unused fireplace.

It became apparent that the indoor gardening virus had invaded my blood and that I would probably never stop acquiring new plants. It was equally clear that the available space would have to be utilized in a more organized and efficient manner.

With no pangs for a vanished dream, the sewing-room and den plans were discarded. Having so many plants to care for, who would have time to read or sew?

The indoor greenhouse-to-be was planned on paper; materials were purchased; benches were built and installed. Soon I had the installation I call my plant factory.

The trivial round, the common task,
Would furnish all we ought to ask.
JOHN KEBLE

2

Furniture for
a Fluorescent Light Garden

The basic equipment needed for a fluorescent light garden consists of something on which to place plants in their containers and light fixtures to suspend over the plants. This is a hobby on which you can spend very little money with an enormous return in fun and satisfaction, or a great deal of money can be spent for gadgets and conveniences if you wish.

Many an item already around the house can be adapted for use in the indoor garden. If, like me, you are cousin to a packrat and never throw anything away because you might be able to use it sometime, someplace, now is the time and your fluorescent light garden is the place. Throughout this book you will find mention of household articles that I have adopted, adapted, or modified for use in my fluorescent light gardens.

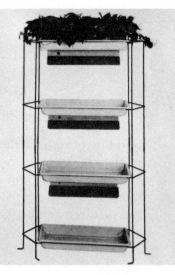

FIG. 8   Evergreen [*Growers Supply Co.*]

FIG. 7   FloraCart [*Tube Craft Co.*]

FIG. 10   Sunlighter [*Tinari Greenhouses*]

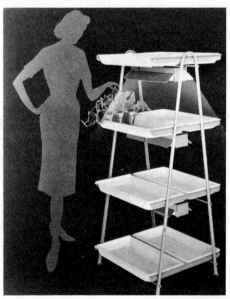

FIG. 9   Grow-Lite Fluorescent Stand
[*Growers Supply Co.*]

READYMADE FURNITURE

If you live in an apartment or in a home that offers no
build-it-yourself facilities, or if you prefer not to be involved
in the construction of the furniture for your fluorescent light
garden, you will find a great range of plant furniture offered
by dealers who specialize in these products. Some of the items
are pictured in this book, and names and addresses of dealers
are in the *Where to Buy* list at the end of the book.

As in many lines of business, there are unscrupulous dealers
who have boarded the indoor gardening bandwagon to cash
in on this very popular hobby. Also, there are some dealers
who in complete innocence are offering equipment that is
unsuitable or of little value to an indoor gardener. The latter
do not intend to cheat; it is just that they are not horticulturists or gardeners themselves, although they may be very
good electricians or manufacturers of fixtures. For example,
I would not buy a fixture or stand that accommodates only one
15- or 20-watt fluorescent lamp with any intention of using it
for the *growing* of plants, because single tube units are inefficient and wasteful sources for fluorescent light culture. Such
a fixture or planter may be useful, however, to *display* a few
plants brought into flower elsewhere, and it is also satisfactory over a small plant-propagating unit. If you attempt a
fluorescent light garden with one small lamp you invite
disappointment.

There are some mighty handsome electrified plant stands
available by mail order, pieces you would not hesitate to place
in your living room. Also, there are strictly utilitarian units
that make no pretense of being attractive. I know of none that
could be called inexpensive, and it would therefore seem wise

FIG. 11   Starlite Garden Lamp [*Floralite Co.*]

FIG. 12   GRO-2202
[*Harvey J. Ridge*]

FIG. 13   Fluorescent Hanging Light [*The House Plant Corner*]

FIG. 14   Gro-Lite PL-52 [*Plant Growth Supplies*]

FIG. 15 Gro-Lite PL-91 [*Acme Lite Products Co.*]

to consider the following before buying: (1) will the stand fit the available space? (2) are the fluorescent light fixtures adjustable in height? (3) if it is a floor model, does the stand have wheels or casters to make moving easy? (4) is it made of a rust-proof or rust-resistant material? and most important (5) does it provide enough light, i.e., 15 to 20 watts of light per square foot of growing area?

BUILD YOUR OWN FURNITURE

If you or someone in your household can build indoor garden furniture, you will be able to use to the best advantage every inch of space in your home that can be allotted to indoor gardening. You can adapt old tables and cabinets and other pieces of tired and retired household furniture that may be lying around in the attic, scrounged from relatives or neighbors, or purchased from a second-hand dealer.

One indoor gardener of my acquaintance got several metal tables on wheels just for removing this condemned equipment from a hospital that was being re-equipped. She removed the tops of the tables, inverted the tops and refastened them to the frames, and had readymade waterproof plant benches on wheels.

The most efficient indoor benches I have ever seen are the triple-deckers such as I have in my plant factory. These were constructed in our home workshop and assembled in the plant room. They reach from floor to ceiling, are free standing and not attached to the building at any point, and strong enough, as we said back in Iowa, to bed down a team of horses. A friend who copied this design declared his benches turned out to be strong enough for only one small pony, but it was all right because he grows only miniature plants. Units of this type can be disassembled easily if they have to be moved.

Our benches consist of 2 by 4 wood frames fastened together with carriage bolts. Bottoms of the benches are made of ½-inch construction grade (also called sheathing grade) plywood, which is run-of-the-mill and less costly than plywood that is finished on one or both sides. The knots and irregularities in this less expensive grade of plywood do not affect its strength, and paint hides the defects. The benches are 8 feet long by 36 inches wide. The distance from one level to the next is 26 inches. The lowest bench is raised 6 inches off the floor. Each tier has two 2-lamp, 8-foot strip flourescent light fixtures except the top one, which has two 2-lamp, 8-foot industrial type fixtures. The fixtures hang by means of sash chain looped over pulleys, balanced by concrete counterweights at each end. The fixtures can be raised and lowered to suit, or kept higher at one end to accommodate tall plants or to provide less light than normal to suit the needs of some plants on the same bench.

A pair of homemade concrete counterweights (one at each end of a fixture) equals the total weight of the fixture with tubes. A 2-tube 96-inch strip fixture with tubes weighs approximately 21 pounds, so each counterweight weighs about 10½ pounds. As there is considerable friction in the sash chain and pulley arrangement, the counterweights can be plus or minus as much as 2 to 3 pounds and still operate satisfactorily. We made our counterweights of a premixed dry concrete aggregate, poured into small cardboard cartons, using a parcel-post scale to weigh out each batch of wet concrete. Wire clothes hangers were embedded for reinforcing and for a loop to hang onto the chain. The blocks were painted with white paint.

The ceiling of the two lower compartments, which is the bottom of the bench above, is painted flat white. At one end

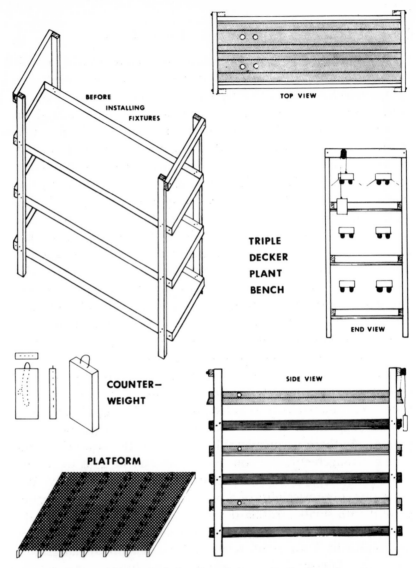

BEFORE
INSTALLING
FIXTURES

TOP VIEW

TRIPLE
DECKER
PLANT
BENCH

END VIEW

COUNTER—
WEIGHT

SIDE VIEW

PLATFORM

FIG. 16   Homemade triple-decker bench in author's plant factory

FIG. 17   Platform. Material required: 7 pieces cedar ¾ by 1½ by 27 inches (stringers), 1 piece wire lath 27 by 32 inches, galvanized staples. Note: no cross pieces—stringers are held only by wire lath.

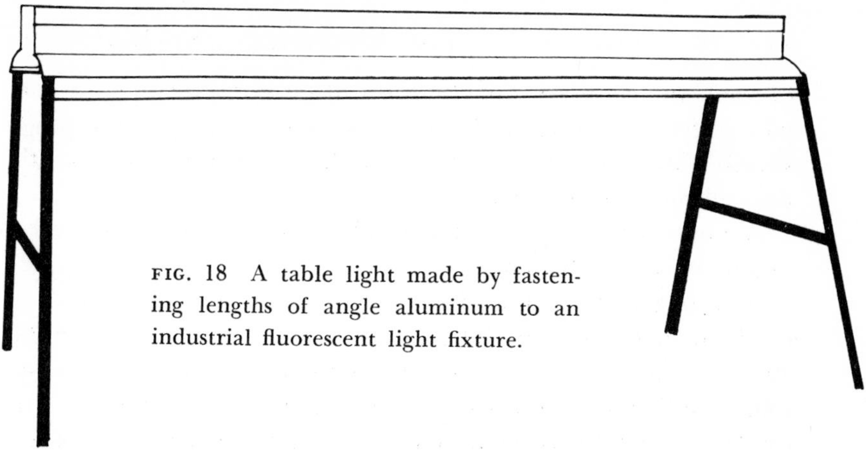

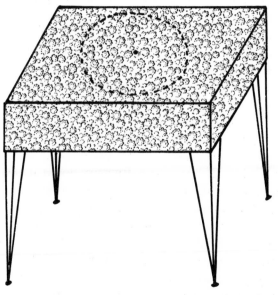

FIG. 18 A table light made by fastening lengths of angle aluminum to an industrial fluorescent light fixture.

FIG. 19 Homemade fixture. Size 16 x 12 x 4 inches, made of ⅜-inch plywood. Inside painted flat white, outside covered with Formica. 22-watt circline fluorescent fixture indicated by dotted line. Wrought iron legs.

of each bench there are double outlets for plugging in each pair of fixtures. The double outlets are connected to the power supply through a time-control switch that is adjustable for the desired on and off periods.

A home safety-type platform ladder of aluminum is used to reach the upper benches.

The benches are lined with plastic. A painter's plastic drop-cloth, which is usually .002 inches (2 mil) thick, used double thick, is fine for this size bench, but it is less expensive to buy plastic sheeting by the roll or bolt. A roll of .004 inch (4 mil) or .005 inch (5 mil) polyethylene or an equivalent transparent or translucent plastic sheeting 100 inches wide by 200 foot long costs about ten dollars at a lumber yard. The plastic lining waterproofs the benches, and prevents water from dripping from one bench onto the light fixtures below it. There is a temptation to staple the plastic sheeting neatly into place as a bench is being lined. Do resist this inclination toward tidiness and mitered corners. A considerable quantity of water can drip through a hole made by a staple in plastic sheeting, even when the staple is in the hole. The plastic should cover the bottom of the bench and come up the sides and over the top, all in one piece with no seams or piecing out.

The benches are filled with builder's coarse vermiculite to a depth of about 2 inches. This is not horticultural vermiculite and must be purchased from a lumber yard or building-supply dealer. A standard bag of insulation fill, 4 cubic feet, is just the right amount for one bench 8 x 3 feet. Zonolite is one brand name of builder's vermiculite.

Humidity is provided in each growth area by keeping the vermiculite wet via the drainage from the pots and by pouring more water on the vermiculite. Several other materials will serve in place of vermiculite—gravel, chicken or turkey grits, crushed oyster shells, stone chips, peat, perlite, sand—but I prefer the coarse vermiculite because it is lightweight and easy to handle. (I would warn, though, that this builder's vermiculite should not be used as or in a potting medium. Several gardeners have found it toxic to plants.)

Before building your benches, check to see how far your arm can reach comfortably, and make the bench width accordingly. We know a slip of a gal whose thoughtful husband built a bench to fill their available space, 36 inches. The bench is against a wall, so she can get at it from just one side. She cannot bear not to use all of the space, and she feels rather silly when she stretches a little beyond her reach and lands face down in the flower pots with no leverage to get back on her feet.

Instead of placing tables or benches around the perimeter of a room, bring them together in pairs in the middle of the room. The two edges that come together will then provide a growing area almost as well lighted as the middle of a single bench, and about a third additional well-lighted growing area is obtained. You still have the same access to each bench as when it is against a wall.

Lengths of aluminum gutters—the kind that get full of leaves outdoors every autumn—can be fastened to the outside edges of benches to increase the growing area. Up to 3-inch pots fit in the gutters nicely.

A beautiful *and* efficient fluorescent light garden was designed by Mrs. William Prescott and is in constant use in her Long Island home. Mrs. Prescott has her garden (it is only one of many fluorescent light gardens in her home) in a room on the second floor, and sometimes moves it to a sunporch. There are four 6-foot by 4-foot shelves. The bottom shelf is on casters. The three top shelves are suspended from ceiling hooks by chains at each of the four corners. The chains run through all three shelves, with each shelf held in place at the desired level by a large pin slipped through a link of the chain.

FIG. 20 African violets, gloxinias, episcias, columneas flower on every shelf of
a four-deck fluorescent light garden suspended from the ceiling. The garden
hangs in a small unused bedroom on
second floor, home of
MRS. WILLIAM F. PRESCOTT.

Each bench is edged with a ¾-inch by 1¾-inch strip of wood, and the whole unit is painted flat white. The benches are plastic lined and filled with chicken grits. Two double strip fluorescent fixtures 12 inches apart are fastened the 6-foot way to the bottom of each bench to light the shelf below. In this setup, lights are fixed permanently in position, and shelves are raised or lowered by moving the supporting pins at the corners to a higher or lower link in the chains. The only annoyance this lovely garden has ever given its owner was when the chicken grits fell through the holes through which the chains run. A little deft hole-plugging with floral clay solved that problem.

PLATFORMS

I do not like to place pots of plants directly on vermiculite or sand. Roots are too quick to grow through drainage holes and into the material on which the pots sit. The roots act as wicks drawing water up into the pots continuously, literally overwatering the plants. Diseases and pests can travel and spread from one infected or infested plant to an entire collection via the vermiculite or any other moisture-retentive material that may be in a bench when all pots rest directly on the material. An infestation may be washed from a pot into the vermiculite, but it will have less chance of getting to other plants if pots are not in direct contact with the vermiculite.

Platforms or stages placed over the vermiculite keep pots from touching what might be a "nematode mine." Platforms must interfere as little as possible with air circulation over the moist medium. It is the evaporation of water from the moist surface that maintains a moist atmosphere for the plants.

I have pressed into service the wire racks taken from an oven and from an old refrigerator; also scrap lengths and

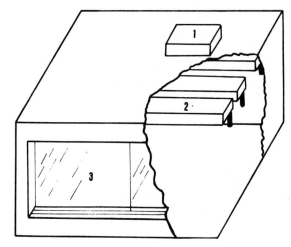

FIG. 21 Homemade enclosed fluorescent light garden.

(1) Ballasts were removed from fixtures and placed outside the box;

(2) single-tube strip fluorescent fixtures;

(3) sliding glass doors.

FIG. 22 Homemade propagating unit. Box is 3 inches deep, 15 inches wide, 24 inches long—must be same length as fixture. 2-tube 20-watt fluorescent light fixture is held 9 inches above the bed by sheet metal

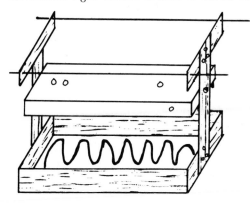

screws. "T" section is 18 inches high, 15 inches wide, 2 stiff wires support plastic sheeting which encloses the unit. Bottom is lined with aluminum foil. 30-watt heating cable is laid on foil and covered with 2 inches of rooting medium.

rectangles of decorative perforated aluminum left over from making a room divider; and wire filing baskets turned upside down. Plastic or metal egg-crate louvers removed from commercial fluorescent fixtures have been used. One of my favorite improvisations is a wrought-iron phonograph record rack which I use for tiny pots of cacti. It hoists the plants well above the moisture in the bench and at the same time puts them closer to the lamps.

Platforms to fit on or in trays or benches can be made of almost any rigid perforated or screenlike material. Two of the best are galvanized plasterer's lath and galvanized hardware cloth, both obtainable at lumber yards.

Plasterer's lath comes in flat sheets 27 inches wide and 96 inches long. The wire pattern is 1/4 inch diamond-shaped. Hardware cloth (sometimes called rabbit wire) is misnamed if anything ever was. It is a wire mesh (1/2-inch mesh is better for this purpose than 1/4-inch) which comes in rolls 24, 30, 36, or 48 inches wide and 25 or 100 feet long. Most lumber yards will cut a few feet of hardware cloth from a big roll for you. Sears Roebuck and Montgomery Ward will take your order for short lengths, too. Both plasterer's lath and hardware cloth can be cut to size and shape with tinsnips or wire cutters and fastened to cedar strips with brads or heavy staples.

Plasterer's lath is rigid enough to be supported by the rims of the benches without being fastened to anything. Plasterer's lath has a couple of advantages over hardware cloth: it is flat, whereas hardware cloth has been rolled and if you happen to get a section from the inside of the roll it is difficult to get the curl out of it; and the lath is about half the price of hardware cloth. Whichever you use, be adamant in demanding the *galvanized* grade—the ungalvanized grades will rust away in no time. Handle both of these materials with care—the raw edges and ends make nasty cuts and scratches.

The platforms in my fluorescent light plant factory are 27-inch by 32-inch pieces of galvanized plasterer's lath (three pieces without waste from a standard 27-inch by 96-inch sheet) stapled to 1½-inch by ¾-inch cedar strips on 7-inch centers. I use these platforms in my greenhouse benches, too.

EQUIPMENT FOR TRAILING AND CLIMBING PLANTS

I have a great fondness for plants that climb or trail. They are not the easiest things in the world to handle in a fluorescent light garden, because their habits of growth keep them on the move and they grow out of the field of light. However, there are several methods of placing and supporting these plants that work well for me.

We built a free-standing bench 8 feet long by 32 inches wide and suspended over it two 8-foot 2-tube industrial fixtures. The fixtures hang on chains from hooks in the ceiling and are raised or lowered by S-hooks fastened in the chains. In the 2-inch space between the two fixtures, a length of chain is suspended from ceiling hooks in several loops. The chain could also be stretched between uprights nailed to each end of the bench, but I find loops from the ceiling more adjustable in height. The hangers on the baskets or pots of trailing plants can be hooked in a link in the center of a loop or in a link higher up on either side of a loop, whatever position is necessary to place the top of the plant a few inches below the tubes. The entire plant is thus exposed to direct and reflected light.

For young plants which will soon develop their inherent training or hanging nature—columneas, episcias, fuchsias, hoyas, ivy-leaved geraniums, ivies, etc.—I suspend a plant rack about 8 or 9 inches directly below the lamps. This can be a piece of ¼-inch plywood in which holes have been cut to insert the

FIG. 23 Exhibit at Long Island Nurserymen's Show of plants grown without sunlight. Plants were loaned to the show by the author and Mrs. William F. Prescott, from their home fluorescent light gardens. Three 20-watt lamps fastened in a triangle on the ceiling make a garden for trailing plants in front of the window at left.

[*Photo by Gottscho-Schleisner, Inc.*]

small pots, or a piece of hardware cloth cut out the same way, or a plastic pot rack such as is sold by Union Products, Inc. I simply loop a piece of fishline or nylon clothesline under each end of the rack and up and over the light fixture, like putting up a child's board swing on a tree branch.

Tall juice cans make good pedestals for pots of trailing plants, but eventually the cans will rust unless given a coat of paint.

There is available at garden centers a wire basket mounted on a three-legged wire frame. The legs lift the bottom of the basket 10 to 12 inches above the bench. Empty, this contraption looks like a wash basin perched on a milking stool, but filled with episcia, tradescantia, or columnea it makes a beautiful verdant cascade on a bench.

The uprights at the corners of double- or triple-decked benches are wonderful for trailing plants in pots. I have pot hooks nailed on all four sides of the uprights of my benches. The outside corners of the uprights receive light from adjacent benches, the inside corners from the lights they face. I usually unsnap these pots from the hooks and carry them to the sink or place them on a bench for watering, as otherwise they would drain onto the floor.

Brackets, the swinging birdcage kind or the rigid kind used for bracing shelves, are good, too, attached to the uprights and supporting hanging baskets.

Garden-Gate Plant Racks (Poulette Welding Co.) are swinging vertical plant holders which were intended for use at windows. I find them ideal for trailing plants when fastened to the corner uprights of benches. You can swing the unit to the lights, where it adds a very pretty touch to the fluorescent light garden, and you can swing it out when you want to work with the plants on the benches.

I handle a lot of my trailing plants by placing the pots at

the edges of the benches and letting the plants trail over the edges and down toward the bench below.

A delightful hanging garden can be installed in a corner in a kitchen or breakfast room with three 20-watt strip fluorescent fixtures arranged in a triangle and baskets or pots suspended from ceiling hooks inside the triangle.

The plants whose nature urges them ever upward get all possible encouragement from me. The pots are placed at the base of the corner uprights of the benches and the plants are trained to creep up, supported where needed with cellophane tape or plastic plant ties. I let the plants branch out and train some of the growth horizontally across the front edges of the benches. Philodendron, climbing ivies, *Ficus pumila (F. repans)* all seem to get enough reflected light in my plant factory to grow well with this treatment. A particular favorite grown in this manner is *Hoya carnosa variegata*. The reflected light is not sufficient to make it flower, so we have installed 4-foot single-tube strip fluorescent fixtures vertically on a couple of the corner uprights, and the wax plant grows right up alongside the light and delights us with its fragrant flower clusters.

Climbing plants can also be trained on trellises, wire frames of every size and form, or totems, inserted in the pot in which the plant grows, and the pot placed on a bench under lights.

3

Fluorescent Light Fixtures and Lamps

FIXTURES

Selecting fluorescent light units to be used for growing plants in quantity is not difficult. Fixtures are pretty much standardized among manufacturers. Although some manufacturers offer certain modifications, basically the choice lies between a fixture with reflectors, called an industrial fixture; or one without reflectors, called a strip, channel, or pan fixture.

The easy way to buy fixtures (and the only way, if you know nothing about electrical wiring and do not want to hire an electrician) is to order them from a manufacturer or dealer who specializes in fixtures for horticultural purposes. The same rules apply to buying fixtures as to buying furniture for your fluorescent light garden: be sure that the fixture will fit the space you have available and that it will provide 15 to 20 watts of fluorescent light per square foot of growing area. On this

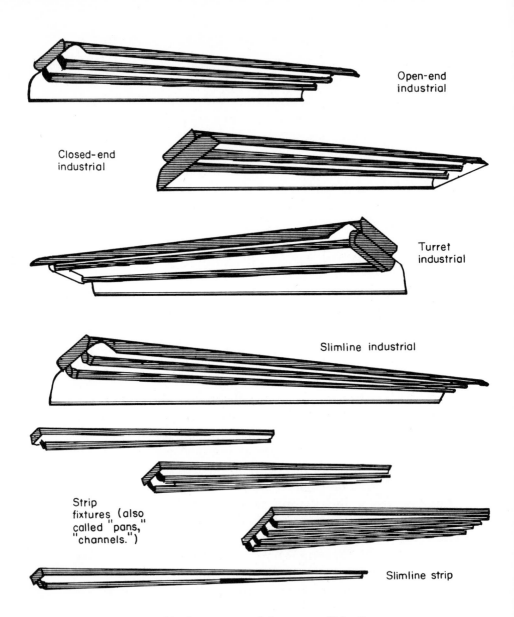

Open-end
industrial

Closed-end
industrial

Turret
industrial

Slimline industrial

Strip
fixtures (also
called "pans,"
"channels.")

Slimline strip

FIG. 24 Some types of fluorescent light fixtures.

basis, a single 40-watt tube will serve a growing area approximately 4 feet long by 6 inches wide.

If you are handy with pliers and screwdriver and know a bare minimum about electrical wiring (you know enough if you can replace a lamp cord or an electric iron cord) your best bet is to buy your fixtures from your local electrical shop or electrical distributor. Usually, all you need do to a fixture purchased this way is to install a cord and plug, hang it up and plug it in. The supplier may even install the cord and plug for a small fee; be sure to tell him the length of cord you need.

A good source of fluorescent light fixtures is the classified section of your daily newspaper. Somebody is always going out of business or installing new fixtures and wanting to sell his old ones at a nominal price. Some of my best buys have been the louvered type of fluorescent fixture (which manufacturers designate as commercials) from small retail shops that were going out of business. Just snap out the plastic shade or louver —the egg-crate type of louver can be used on the bench as a platform for pots—and you have an industrial fixture, i.e., a fixture with reflectors.

In light output, the industrial and the strip fixture are about equal, size for size. In price, the strip fixture costs a little less. The industrials usually have built-in hooks or clamps to facilitate hanging, whereas the strips need a hook or clamp screwed or bolted on.

The purpose of using fluorescent lights for indoor gardening is to get enough light to enable plants to grow and flower. The plants receive light directly from the fluorescent tube, and also by reflection. The industrial type of fixture, that is, one with reflectors, should be used where there will be nothing immediately above the fixture to act as a reflector. The strip type of fixture, with no reflectors, should be used in and under cabinets and shelves, where the surface to which it is fastened can be painted white to act as a reflector. Reflectors can be mounted behind or fastened to strip fixtures if desired. Most fixture manufacturers make reflectors for this purpose; or it is a simple matter to make your own by cutting the required size from a piece of sheet aluminum (available at hardware stores in 36-inch squares). The aluminum can be cut with tinsnips or household scissors and painted white.

The most commonly available sizes of both industrial and strip fixtures are 1-tube, 2-tube, 3-tube, and 4-tube units that will accommodate 20-watt (24-inch) lamps, 40-watt (48-inch) lamps, or 72-, 73-, 74- or 75-watt (96-inch) lamps. Fixtures are usually a little longer than the tubes, just how much depends on the individual manufacturer. If space is tight, play it safe and assume that the fixtures will be about 2 inches longer than the tubes, when you are planning.

There are other sizes, shapes, and descriptions of fluorescent fixtures available, but unless you have a special space or decorating problem, it is best to standardize on those mentioned above. There are fixtures for 14-watt (15-inch) tubes, 15-watt (18-inch) tubes, 25-watt (33-inch) tubes, 30-watt (36-inch) tubes, and others. They are usually hard to find and the tubes that fit them may have to be purchased on special order—no help at all when you need a lamp in a hurry. It is my experience that a tube of less than 40 watts is inefficient and wasteful for growing plants. If you must use a fixture of a size that holds other than 40-watt or 72-watt tubes, adhere as closely as possible to the rule of 15 to 20 watts of light per square foot of growing area, plus or minus very little.

Light output falls off at both ends of a fluorescent tube—*any* fluorescent tube—due to the internal construction and the blackening due to use. It is best, therefore, to use the longest fixture possible. If you have, say, 100 inches in length to illu-

TABLE I.

GROWING AREAS LIGHTED BY TUBULAR FLUORESCENT LAMPS

Length of lamp	Number of lamps	Lamp wattage	Approx. growing area in sq. ft.	Approx. size of growing area
24"	1	20 watt	1	24" x 6"
24"	2	20 watt end to end	2	48" x 6"
24"	2	20 watt side by side	2	24" x 12"
48"	1	40 watt	2	48" x 6"
48"	2	40 watt end to end	4	96" x 6"
48"	2	40 watt side by side	4	48" x 12"
48"	3	40 watt end to end	6	144" x 6"
48"	3	40 watt side by side	6	48" x 18"
48"	4	40 watt end to end	8	192" x 6"
48"	4	40 watt side by side	8	48" x 24"
96"	1	72 watt	4	96" x 6"
96"	2	72 watt end to end	8	192" x 6"
96"	2	72 watt side by side	8	96" x 12"
96"	3	72 watt side by side	12	96" x 18"
96"	4	72 watt side by side	16	96" x 24"

minate, use one fixture with 96-inch tubes rather than two fixtures with 48-inch tubes end to end.

The fixtures you will use in fluorescent light gardens operate on 115 volt, 60 cycle house current, the same as your household appliances. When planning your installation, be sure that your electrical system will carry the additional load you plan to put on it. A normal house circuit will carry about 1500 watts safely. Figuring that the ballasts (these control devices are described on page 43) use 10 watts for every 40 watts of light, you could safely have thirty 40-watt tubes (1200 watts) and their ballasts (300 watts) on one circuit in your house, provided nothing else is on that circuit.

In all 20-watt and 40-watt fixtures, you will find a choice of "preheat" or "rapid start." Buy the preheat; they usually cost a little less, and rapid start fixtures may give starting trouble under the high humidity conditions necessary for growing plants. In the 72-, 73-, 74- or 75-watt (96-inch) size, buy the slimline type of fixture which uses a single-pin base.

A circline fluorescent fixture works well in small, square areas, such as shadow boxes. Circlines are usually available in polished chrome or white finish fixtures (buy the white for better reflection of light) and in three sizes, as listed in Table II.

TABLE II.

GROWING AREAS LIGHTED BY CIRCLINE FLUORESCENT LAMPS

Diameter of fixture	Lamp size	Will light a garden area of
8½″	22 watt	1 square foot (12″ x 12″)
12½″	32 watt	2 square feet (about 18″ x 18″)
12½″	Combination of one 22 watt and one 32 watt	3 square feet (about 21″ x 21″)
16½″	40 watt	2 square feet (about 18″ x 18″)
16½″	Combination of one 32 watt and one 40 watt	4 square feet (about 24″ x 24″)

HOW A FLUORESCENT LAMP PRODUCES LIGHT

At each end of the lamp is an electrode, consisting of an oxide-coated coil of tungsten wire, called a filament. When heated by an electrical current, the filament releases a cloud of electrons around each electrode. A high voltage electrical surge passing between the electrodes then establishes an arc stream of electrons which travels back and forth between the two electrodes with the alternations of the current. These electrons, as they shuttle back and forth within the glass tube, col-

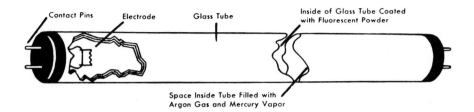

FIG. 25 How a fluorescent lamp produces light.

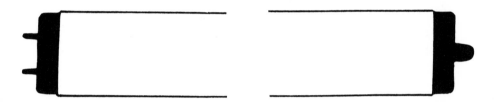

FIG. 26 Fluorescent lamp bases. Left, medium bi-pin base. Right, single-pin base.

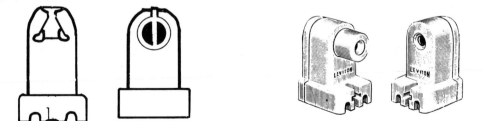

FIG. 27 Fluorescent lamp sockets. Left, two types of sockets for bi-pin lamps. Right, a pair of sockets for single-pin lamps.

lide with atoms of mercury vapor and argon gas that occupy the lamp tube, producing mostly *invisible* ultraviolet rays. The ultraviolet rays excite the fluorescent powders that coat the inside surface of the tube, causing them to glow and emit *visible* light.

As you will learn in the next chapter, ultraviolet light is not beneficial for growing plants. However, the amount of ultraviolet light that escapes from a fluorescent lamp is minute, and the only disagreeable thing I have found about it is that this invisible light attracts certain insects tiny enough to get through the finest window screen in the summertime. Whether we like it or not, the ultraviolet light has to be in the fluorescent light tube to make it fluoresce.

TYPES OF LAMPS

There are three types of fluorescent lamps:

1. The *preheat* lamp, in which the cathodes must be momentarily preheated before the lamp will light. This requires the use of a "starter," that operates only during the starting period. The use of a starter increases lamp life because a lower open circuit voltage can be used, and allows the use of a less expensive ballast. The standard bi-pin connection allows current to flow through the cathodes for preheating. Generally, the preheat lamps are the most economical of all fluorescent lamps to operate due to long lamp life, high light output and low-cost ballast. Preheat lamps are available in the following sizes: 15-watt (18-inch), 20-watt (24-inch), 30-watt (36-inch), and 40-watt (48-inch) which is the largest preheat lamp made. Starters do burn out and wear out. Buy FS-2 starters for 15- and 20-watt lamps, and FS-4 starters for 30- and 40-watt lamps.

These starter designations are universal among all starter manufacturers.

2. The *rapid start* lamp, which requires no starter; the filament is continuously heated during operation, at low voltage. Full operation of the lamp is achieved in one or two seconds. The ballasts required are smaller and quieter. Rapid start lamps are available in 30-watt (36-inch) and 40-watt (48-inch) sizes only. Rapid start lamps are versatile—they will serve in either preheat or rapid start fixtures.

3. The *slimline instant start* lamp that requires no starter because filament preheating or heating during operation is not necessary due to the use of higher voltage ballasts. Lamps start without delay. The slimline instant start lamp has a single-pin base for quick insertion in push-pull sockets. In the 8-foot lengths they are the most efficient lamps available. They will light a given area with just half the number of fixtures and lamps required for customary 4-foot fixtures. Slimline instant start lamps are available in many lengths and wattages. The wattage rating is slightly different from other fluorescent lamps. A 24-inch lamp is 21 watts; a 48-inch lamp is 39 watts; a 96-inch lamp is 73 watts. Slimline instant start lamps require slimline instant start fixtures. If I were starting my fluorescent light gardens from the beginning, I would use only slimline instant start fixtures and lamps.

In the 40-watt (48-inch) size only, there is a slimline instant start lamp of medium bi-pin construction. It looks like a preheat or rapid start lamp, but is not interchangeable with them and requires a special ballast.

OTHER TYPES OF FLUORESCENT LAMPS

When your fluorescent light garden is all set up, operating beautifully, and delighting you with flowers, if your luck is anything like mine a friend of a friend is bound to come along and ask you why you are not using some kind of lamp or fixture that you never heard of before. Your friend's nosey friend will probably talk to you about high output lamps, very high output lamps, powertubes, powergroove lamps, powertwist lamps, and others that *sound* perfectly marvelous for growing plants.

It is true, these lamps produce more light per foot of lamp, using the same size fixtures, than the conventional lamps that I advise.

You should send your friend's friend packing for two reasons: (1) you do not *need* all that extra light (and naturally it costs more) except in very special installations; and (2) by the time you find a dealer who can sell you the one or two lamps you would want, you will be too old to care. They definitely are not something you can pick up at the corner hardware store.

Another suggestion that will be made to you sooner or later is that you should use fluorescent lamps with a built-in reflector. This so-called reflector consists of a reflecting coating silvered on the inside for a part of the circumference of the tube. Save your money—the output of light of reflector lamps is no greater than that of a conventional fluorescent lamp mounted in a standard industrial or strip fixture.

BALLASTS

All fluorescent lamps require ballasts. The ballast is the control device which limits the current to the proper operating value. A fluorescent lamp is fundamentally an electrical discharge source and its current would rise to a value that would destroy the lamp, unless controlled.

The ballast must be designed for the specific size and type of lamp used, as well as for the voltage and frequency of the electrical system. It is necessary to use the correct ballast for each kind of lamp, to prevent filament damage, which may cause burnout.

Two types of ballasts are available: the *low-power factor* ballast and the *high-power factor* ballast. Although the wiring differs slightly, they produce the same end results, are interchangeable, and either may be replaced with the other, provided, of course, they have the same electrical characteristics. The difference between them is in economy of operation. The high-power factor ballast consumes less electricity than the low-power factor ballast to produce the same amount of light. When lamps are burned for long periods, say the 12 to 16 hours a day required for growing plants, the slight extra initial cost of a high power factor ballast is justified by the saving in power costs during the life of the ballast. The life of a ballast is unpredictable; we have several that have been in operation for twenty years, and we have also had a ballast burn out in a week.

The humming sound that is sometimes emitted by a fluorescent fixture comes from the ballast in the fixture. It is caused by loose laminations in the ballast that occur during the manufacturing process. It is undesirable but involves no danger. Most manufacturers rate their ballasts on a noise-level basis: the ballasts are tested on the production line, and the noisiest ones become the least expensive, the quietest ones the most expensive. If you are sensitive to this humming sound (and frankly, it irritates me beyond endurance sometimes) you can stipulate to your electrical supplier that you must have ballasts of the lowest noise rating in your fixtures. However, I have found that high-power factor ballasts are generally quiet enough, even for a writer who can be distracted by the sound of a leaf falling from a plant in the next room!

Ballasts are power-consuming devices and naturally they give off heat. We can say, with truth, that fluorescent lamps are cool and will not burn plants, but somebody always reminds us that he can indeed feel heat around a fluorescent light fixture. The heat comes not from the lamps but from the ballasts. To prevent ballasts from overheating, a certain amount of ventilation is required. Standard fixtures are proportioned so that the metal body of the fixture will radiate a sufficient amount of ballast heat under normal conditions. Fixtures installed in an enclosed box or case may not receive enough natural ballast ventilation and the fixtures may overheat; also the ballast heat that builds up inside the case may be too much for the plants. In an installation of this kind, ballasts can be removed from fixtures and located outside the box at a distance of up to 5 feet away from the fixture; this should be done by an electrician.

If a ballast burns out, replace it with a high-power factor ballast. Do not discard a fixture just because the ballast goes. Replacing ballasts is a simple procedure and a lot cheaper than buying a new fixture. Most quality ballasts have a wiring diagram on the ballast case—be sure to follow the diagram when replacing the burned out ballast.

SWITCHES

Although you may use a time-clock switch to turn your fluorescent lights on and off, each fixture should be equipped with an individual on-off switch.

There are two types of switches from which to choose, one that is installed in the fixture or one that is installed in the connecting cord. The latter is called an "in-line" switch.

The preferred way is to have a switch installed in the fixture. Most industrial and strip fixtures have a ⅜″ knockout hole in the ends or sides for inserting a switch. (There is usually a larger knockout hole nearby, which is intended for cable.) You have a choice of switches: pull-chain, toggle, rotary, or push type. All are good—select the type you like best.

If a switch installed directly in the fixture is impractical for you, use an in-line switch in the connecting wire. These in-line switches are installed very easily in the lamp cord and are available at most local hardware stores. If you are not handy with tools, it might be a good idea to have the switches installed where you buy your fixtures.

HOW TO INSTALL A FLUORESCENT LAMP IN A FIXTURE

The base of a fluorescent lamp is the metal or plastic cap and prongs (called "pins") at the end, and every fluorescent lamp except a circline has two bases.

There are two kinds of bases: bi-pin and single-pin, the latter being found on slimline instant start lamps. A bi-pin lamp cannot be used in a single-pin socket, and a single-pin lamp cannot be used in a bi-pin socket.

Switch off the power to the fixture before you install lamps.

Bi-pin sockets. Two types of sockets are employed on fixtures which use lamps having medium bi-pin bases.

One type has a vertical slot into which both pins are inserted and the tube given a quarter turn about its own axis to lock it in place.

The other type has in effect a triangular shaped recess, with an opening at the apex. The tube is inserted with the pins at an angle until the upper pins (one at each end of the lamp) engage one of the contacts. The tube is then given about a one-third turn with the engaged pin as the center of rotation, until both pins at both ends are engaged by both contacts at both ends. Lamps are removed by reversing this procedure.

Care should be exercised that the pins at each end of the tube are properly aligned in the sockets before turning the lamp into position, otherwise improper connections may result, or in severe cases pins may be broken.

A medium bi-pin based lamp will work in either of the two kinds of bi-pin sockets interchangeably, as long as the sockets at both ends of the fixture are the same.

The type of sockets used in fixtures is the manufacturer's choice and the customer usually may not specify. Sockets are available at most hardware stores. If a socket is damaged do not hesitate to replace it; just remember that the sockets at both ends of the fixture must be of the same design.

In most fluorescent fixtures with starters, the starter socket is attached to one of the lamp sockets. To install a starter, push the protruding points which are located at one end of the starter into the large part of the starter socket connection holes and give the starter a slight twist to the right to lock it in place. The starter may go in at a slight angle or feel loose in its socket—this is normal and of no danger; it must make only a slight contact and does not have to fit snugly. Unless it is damaged, it is not necessary to replace the starter socket when replacing a lamp socket. It can be removed easily from the old lamp socket and attached to the new socket.

Single-pin sockets. Slimline instant start lamps have only one contact pin at each end and therefore use sockets quite different from those used by bi-pin lamps. Slimlines use a single hole socket at each end of the fixture. The socket at one end is rigid; the socket at the other end is spring loaded so it can be pushed back against the spring tension when inserting the lamp. One end of the lamp (either end) is inserted in the spring-loaded socket and pushed back as far as possible. The other end of the lamp is then brought up into line with the rigid socket and allowed to be pushed into the socket by means of the spring tension from the socket at the other end. Lamps are removed by reversing this procedure. This type of socket is sometimes called a push-pull socket.

As in the case of bi-pin sockets, slimline sockets can be replaced easily if damaged; however, the chances of a damaged slimline socket are remote—we have never encountered one in many years of use.

Both slimline and bi-pin *lamps* are interchangeable end for end, so do not worry about which end of the lamp goes in which end of the fixture. Use care when installing tubes, and be sure that the lamps are properly aligned in the sockets at each end before completing the insertion procedure.

HOW TO FIGURE THE TOTAL WATTAGE OF A FLUORESCENT LIGHT INSTALLATION

Lamps operating on their proper electrical characteristics consume their rated wattage. A 2-lamp ballast uses about one fourth the wattage of the two lamps it controls. Two 40-watt lamps with their 2-lamp ballast will use together about 100 watts. A single lamp ballast will use about one third the number of watts as the lamp it controls.

THE LIFE AND LIGHT OUTPUT OF A FLUORESCENT LAMP

When I started gardening with fluorescent lights, conventional fluorescent lamps were rated for a service life of 5,000 hours. That life expectancy has been increased by 50 per cent. The manufacturers are constantly increasing the longevity of their lamps. Conventional fluorescent lamps now are generally rated for a service life of 7,500 hours. This rating is based on the manufacturer's assumption that a lamp will be burned three hours each time it is started. However, the life of a fluorescent lamp is greatly affected by the frequency with which it is started. The longer it burns per start, the more economically it will operate and the longer it will last.

A lamp that is rated for 7,500 hours of light when it is burned for three hours per start will give 12,500 hours of service when burned for 14 hours per start, 13,500 hours when burned for 18 hours per start, and 18,700 hours if it is burned continuously from the first time it is started.

A fluorescent lamp will burn and give light for its rated service life, and probably longer, before it fails. However, its light output, or brightness, depreciates as the lamp ages. Light output decreases rather rapidly during the first 100 hours of operation, about 10 per cent. Therefore, for rating purposes, the 100-hour value is used. (You will probably observe that your plants surge when you install a new lamp—a new lamp is initially 10 per cent brighter than it will be after 100 hours of use). At the 500 hour point, there is approximately a 5 per cent depreciation from the rated output; and, on the average, light output depreciates 20 to 30 per cent from rated output by the end of the lamp's rated life.

It is difficult to get anyone but an illuminating engineer to acknowledge it, but the fluorescent powders or phosphors that coat the inside of a fluorescent tube become redder as a lamp ages, having an effect on the *color* of light the plants receive (color of light is discussed in the next chapter). For this reason, and because of the depreciation in light output, the lamps in a fluorescent light garden should be replaced when they reach about 80 per cent of their rated service life, or when dark rings appear at the ends of the tubes, whichever comes first.

TABLE III.

FLUORESCENT LAMP REPLACEMENT CHART

Hours burned per day on 1 start	Average Service Life in hours	80% of average Service Life (replacement time)
10	11,200	8,960 hrs. (896 days or approx. 2.5 yrs.)
12	12,000	9,600 hrs. (800 days or approx. 2.2 yrs.)
14	12,500	10,000 hrs. (714 days or just under 2 yrs.)
16	13,000	10,400 hrs. (650 days or approx. 1.8 yrs.)
18	13,500	10,800 hrs. (600 days or approx. 1.7 yrs.)

I do not recommend a mass replacement program, where all the lamps in a fluorescent light garden would be replaced at the same time. If your plants could talk, they would probably holler good and loud at being subjected abruptly to so much brilliance. In a situation where all of your lamps are ready for replacement at the same time, replace them one or two at a time about a week apart.

I write the installation date and the calculated replacement date on the glass, near the base of the lamp, with a grease pencil, and take care not to wash it off when I clean the lamps.

CAUSES AND SYMPTOMS OF LAMP FAILURE

Besides frequent starting, other factors that affect the life of a fluorescent lamp are low voltage, improperly timed starters, cold temperatures, and faulty ballasts.

Fluorescent lamps give their best performance when the room temperature is between 60 and 90 degrees F. Light output decreases at either lower or higher temperatures.

As a lamp ages, general darkening along the entire length of the tube occurs as a normal condition, due to mercury streaking. You may not even notice this gradual darkening until you compare a lamp that has burned for over a thousand hours with a brand-new one. Under normal conditions, there is little indication of blackening during the first 1,000 hours or so of operation.

Heavy blackening at the ends of the tube may occur from material given off by the electrodes and indicates that the end of the lamp's life is near. Premature end blackening, before a lamp has given a proper length of service, may be due to improper starting, frequent starting with short operating periods, improper ballast equipment, unusual high or low voltages, improper wiring, or a defective lamp. Whatever the cause of the end blackening, and at whatever point in the lamp's age it may occur, it means the lamp will soon fail, and it should be replaced.

End blackening should not be confused with a mercury deposit which sometimes condenses around the bulb at the ends. Occasionally it is visible on new lamps, but should evaporate after the lamp has been in operation for some time. It may reappear when the lamp cools. Frequently, dark streaks appear lengthwise of the tube due to small globules of mercury cooling on the lower (cooler) part of the lamp. Mercury may condense at any place on the tube if a cold object is allowed to lie against the tube for a short period, and such spots near the center section may not again evaporate. Rotating the lamp 180 degrees in the lampholders may give a more favorable position for evaporation.

Near the end of life, some lamps may develop a very dense spot about $\frac{1}{2}$ inch wide and extending almost half way around the tube, centering about 1 inch in from the base. This is normal, but should such a spot develop early in life, it is an indication of excessive starting or operating current.

Occasionally, a lamp may develop a ring or gray band at one end or both, about 2 inches from either base. These rings have no effect on lamp performance and do not indicate that lamp failure is near.

The light in a new fluorescent tube may "barber pole," "snake," or otherwise wave around in the tube. This is normal and will stop as the tube seasons.

Older lamps that flash on and off are nearing the end of their use. Flashing in newer lamps may be caused by improper wiring with the leads "crisscrossed" so that the starter socket of one lamp is connected to the lampholder of the other. Defective starters or ballasts, low voltage, low temperatures, or defective lamps also may account for flashing.

Fluorescent lamps are not so sensitive to voltage variations as incandescent lamps, but they must be operated within the voltage range specified on the ballast for proper performance. Low voltage decreases light output and lamp life, makes starting uncertain, and causes excessive blackening of tubes. High voltage also shortens lamp life, causes severe blackening and may overheat the ballast and cause it to fail. There is absolutely nothing you can do about a temporary low or high voltage condition in your power supply, except replace the lamps and equipment that may be damaged, as you would have to do with electric motors or other electric equipment damaged in the same way in your home. Voltage is controlled by the power company and is influenced by the amount of power being consumed in the area at a given time. The power company is as unhappy as you and I are when a momentary low voltage condition occurs.

Just as we should not always blame the seedsman or nurseryman when a plant fails to grow for us, so we should not assume that a fluorescent lamp that fails prematurely is a defective lamp. Any of the several malfunctions listed above could be responsible for burning out a good lamp.

WHEN LAMPS ARE SLOW TO START

Instant-start and rapid-start lamps sometimes give difficulty in starting in a fluorescent light garden—they just do not light up as instantaneously as they are supposed to. This is because the conditions of high humidity necessary in a good garden allow moisture to collect on the outside of the glass when the lights are off. The moisture momentarily affects the insulating properties of the glass envelope. The condition is easily corrected by applying a coating of silicones, which removes the existing moisture from the tube and prevents further moisture from forming.

It is now standard practice for lamp manufacturers to apply a silicone coating to fluorescent lamps during the manufacturing process, to assure dependable performance under extreme conditions. The coating is sometimes disturbed during shipping or storage, and it inevitably is removed when a lamp is washed or cleaned.

Clean the tubes thoroughly and recoat with a very thin

coating of a material that contains silicones, using a soft cloth. Several furniture polishes—Pledge, Endust, Tone—and at least one window spray cleaner—Easy Off—are excellent for this do-it-yourself silicone coating job. It is part of my maintenance routine to wipe the lamps with one of the products mentioned every time I clean them.

TIME CONTROL SWITCH

A plug-in time control switch should be included in your plans. It will turn the lights on and off automatically at the same time every day. A good time control switch, or timer, will have an Underwriters Laboratory (UL) label, carry at least 1500 watts, and be easily adjusted over the entire 24 hour range. I use and can recommend Paragon, Tork, and General Electric timers, and there are other good ones.

TIPS ON FIXTURES AND LAMPS

1. Clean tubes and fixtures at least once a month, to keep the light output at the highest possible level. Anything, including dust and grime, that gets between the lamp and the plants cuts down on the efficiency of the lamp. Dirty fixtures waste instead of reflecting light.

2. When painting a surface for maximum light reflection, use *flat white* paint, not gloss. Our eyes deceive us on this point, but flat white has a better coefficient of reflection than gloss white and should be used when maximum reflection of light is desired. 'Tis said that one lives in hope and dies in despair, and I have given up hoping that fluorescent fixture manufacturers will ever put anything but a baked enamel finish on their

FIG. 28 Table fountain with recirculating pump.

[*Jerry Priplata*]

FIG. 29 (*Opposite*) Intermatic Time-All automatic timer switch.

[*The House Plant Corner*]

FIG. 31 General Electric footcandle light meter.

[*The House Plant Corner*]

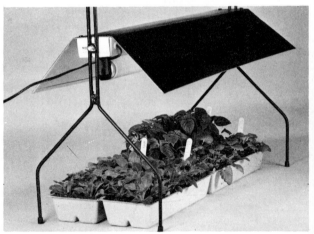

FIG. 30 Bedding Plant Kit. [*Geo. W. Park Seed Co.*]

fixtures. I get rid of it fast by wiping the fixture with a material from the paint store (Wil-Bond is one brand name) that conditions a painted surface to accept another coat of paint, and then I put on a coat of flat white paint, usually from an aeresol can.

The shininess of an aluminum surface deceives the eye, too. Aluminum oxidizes (tarnishes), and the more it becomes tarnished the more light it absorbs and the less it reflects. Spraying aluminum with a clear plastic coating to prevent oxidizing kills the reflection qualities of aluminum. The only thing to do with an aluminum reflector to prevent oxidizing and to get the best reflection of light is to paint it with flat white paint.

3. For maximum reflection of light, do not use a fixture with slots or perforations in the reflector that allow some of the light to escape upward or outward. A perforated or slotted fixture, however, is pretty when used decoratively over plants that are on display.

4. Do not buy bargain fluorescent tubes of an unknown manufacturer, even though these tubes sometimes *appear* to be brighter than those offered by reputable manufacturers at higher prices. All a manufacturer has to do to make tubes appear brighter is use more green phosphors in the inside coating of the tube. The green light does little or nothing for the growing plants, and the fluorescent powders used to produce the green light deteriorate faster than do the other colors of powders. Bargain lamps may prove to be quite costly.

5. If a tube fails to light, or flashes or clicks on and off, check the starter—it is the most likely source of this kind of trouble.

6. To reduce the intensity of fluorescent light, raise the fixture, lower the plant, or suspend one or more layers of cheesecloth or nylon netting (buy the latter in the yard goods section of a department store) directly under the tubes.

7. Replace the lamps in a fluorescent light garden according

to the Lamp Replacement Chart (Table III), or when dark rings appear at the ends of the tubes, whichever comes first.

8. Fluorescent *lamps* are not damaged by splashed water, but do not get water in the *sockets* or *inside the fixtures,* lest you short-circuit the fixtures.

9. Follow the rule of providing 15 to 20 watts of light per square foot of growing area. 15 watts is the bare minimum for a square foot—come as close to 20 watts as you can.

PART TWO

The Environment

Accuse not Nature! she hath done her part;
Do thou but thine!

God saw the Light was good;
And light from darkness by the hemisphere
Divided: Light the Day, and Darkness Night,
He named. Thus was the first Day even and morn.

JOHN MILTON

4

Light

We are blessed to be living on an earth that is energized by a sun. To my ears the very word, light, is one of the most beautiful words in any language.

THE NATURE OF LIGHT

The light from the sun is the source of the world's energy. Without the sun there would be frigid and eternal darkness. There would be no life at all, because there would be no plants and without plants, there would be no food. Life on the planet Earth depends on a process called photosynthesis, which means *manufacture by light*. This process takes place only in the green parts of plants. A plant leaf is a factory that captures the energy of light, enabling it to absorb carbon dioxide from the air and combine it with water absorbed by the plant's roots to make carbohydrates. These are the chemical substances from which all other foods and all parts of all living cells are made.

Light enables us to see by stimulating certain nerves in the

back of the eye. Light warms the earth and this heating of the
earth causes the convection currents called wind, which is
energy in motion. Light can cause motion directly because it
exerts a tiny push when it strikes an object; it causes the chemical changes in many things such as photographic films that
enable us to take pictures. Light can be converted into electrical
energy. Light is a marvelous form of energy, the subject of study
for hundreds of years. From these studies by scientists have
come many useful optical devices which we now consider neces-
sities of modern life, such as cameras, eyeglasses, telescopes,
microscopes, projectors.

Most of us have seen the colors into which the white light
of the sun is broken when it passes through a prism or a piece
of cut glass. At least we have all seen a rainbow. We are familiar,
therefore, with the so-called colors of the solar spectrum. We
know that the visible colors are violet, blue, green, yellow,
orange, and red. The rays we can *see* are only a portion of
those that reach the earth from the sun. There are additional
solar radiations such as ultraviolet rays, x-rays, gamma rays,
infrared rays, and others, which are invisible.

Everything under the sun *receives* all of the sun's light rays,
but the different forms of life—people, animals, insects, plants
—do not *utilize* the same light rays or combinations of rays.
The human eye sees most efficiently in the green/yellow area of
the visible color spectrum. From the invisible range people
absorb the infrared rays to warm themselves and the ultraviolet
rays to tan their skins. Plants make various uses of parts of the
solar spectrum at various stages in their life cycle: germination,
growth, flowering, and dormancy. Plant leaves absorb principally the red and blue light and, it is now believed, probably
very little of the yellow/green light is utilized by plants although
it is so important for human vision.

THE EFFECT OF LIGHT ON PLANT GROWTH

The relationship of light to plant growth has been explored by plant scientists and discoveries of intricate reactions have been published in numerous scientific reports. But plant scientists "still regard the interior of growing plants as a dark continent to a considerable extent." *

Marvelous discoveries have been made through endless experiments. The plant scientists in the U. S. Department of Agriculture have contributed greatly to our knowledge since 1918, when two USDA scientists discovered that some plants wait for short days to form seed, and that plants differ in the day-lengths required for seed formation, flowering, and other movements in the life cycle.

Light: shall it be present or absent? what color? what intensity? of what duration? Each stage in the life cycle of each plant on earth requires a personal answer. The scientists believe that their progress in finding the answers in the coming quarter-century will outpace that of the last hundred years. It is not unreasonable to expect that before the end of the twentieth century we may understand how and why plants grow as they do on an earth irradiated by the sun.

We know enough now, however, about the photoreactions of plants to enable us, without sunlight or with inadequate daylight, to grow ornamental plants indoors with success and great pleasure, by the manipulation of fluorescent light.

In performing their unique function of converting light energy into chemical compounds, plants store energy for future use. Chlorophyll—as plentiful as sand but more valuable than

* *Plant Light-Growth Discoveries,* ARS 22-64, Agricultural Research Service, United States Department of Agriculture, January 1961.

gold—is the key to the existence of life. It is the green stuff in all vegetative matter—stems, leaves, branches, etc.—which captures and uses the sun's energy to convert air and water by photosynthesis into sugars and starches. Light is the only form of energy, so far as we know, that will initiate this process. Plants (unlike people, animals, and machines) can use the energy of the sun directly, and can store this energy for future use. By photosynthesis, plants produce enough sugars and starches not only to support their own life and promote their own growth, but enough to produce energy for their own reproduction. Dead plants store enough energy to provide food for people and animals, and in the form of coal, petroleum, natural gas and other remnants of vegetable life to provide light, heat, and power for homes and industry.

PHOTOREACTIONS OF PLANTS

The response of plants to the relative lengths of periods of darkness and periods of light is called *photoperiodism,* a name coined by W. W. Garner and H. A. Allard of the USDA who discovered that some plants wait for short days to form seed. Plants that flower in response to longer days than nights are called *long-day* plants; those that respond to shorter days than nights are *short-day* plants; those that will flower and fruit under a wide range of day lengths are called *indeterminate* or *daylength-neutral;* those that respond to days and nights of approximately equal length are called *intermediate.* A "long-day" plant would more accurately be termed a "short-night" plant, and a "short-day" plant should be called a "long-night" plant, because plants measure the dark period in a 24-hour cycle. So far as is known now, they do not clock their light periods. However, the terms introduced at the time of the discovery of photoperiodism have become a part of the language and are continued for consistency.

The response of plants whereby the direction of growth is determined not only by the quantity and quality of light but also by the direction from which the light comes is called *phototropism*. Stems of plants grow toward light, and their phototropism is *positive; negative* phototropism has been observed in the roots of certain plants. *Transverse* phototropism describes the action of leaves which grow perpendicular to the direction of the light.

Plants unceasingly adjust themselves in relation to the light available to them, to expose the maximum amount of their green matter. They bend toward the light. During periods of weak light, chloroplasts (the specks which contain the chlorophyll) adjust themselves to absorb as much as possible of the available light. During periods of very strong illumination, which might destroy the chlorophyll, the chloroplasts turn their sides to the light to protect the chlorophyll from overexposure, always moving to give the most efficient photosynthesis. This movement is called *phototaxis* (the Greek *taxis* meaning arrangement).

Growth reactions in the stems and leaves of plants in which the reaction is *caused* by light but is *due only* to the construction of the stems and leaves is called *photonasty* (denoting a change in position in a specified direction).

The reaction of light on a plant pigment called *phytochrome* (from the Greek *phyton* meaning a plant, and *chroma* meaning color or colored) triggers the starting and stopping of plant growth. Phytochrome was detected in plants in the early 1950's by scientists in the USDA Agricultural Research Service; in 1959 they were able to isolate the chemical for study, and coined the name when the achievement was announced.

There is a relationship between light and heat in light's

effect on plant growth. Heat in the degree required by the individual plant must be present to permit light to set off its various photoreactions.

Although we do not know yet all of the ways in which light affects the growth of plants, plant scientists have discovered that, theoretically at least, the best plant growth can be obtained from a source of light which is rich in the violet/blue part of the visible color spectrum, has little of the green/yellow area, and is rich in the orange/red portion.

Light in the violet/blue area does two things: it stimulates the plant mechanism which compels it to grow in the direction of the light (phototropism), and it promotes the production of sugars and starches in the plant's green matter (photosynthesis).

Light in the green/yellow area (the light most efficient for human vision) apparently has little effect on plants one way or the other, although this is still to be proven. The chlorophyll *absorbs* the red and blue light, but *reflects* the yellow and green light, giving the leaves the appearance we call green.

Light in the orange/red area appears to perform two functions: it triggers the plant material (phytochrome) which causes germination and plant growth; and, like blue light, it promotes the production of plant food (photosynthesis).

The complete effect of invisible infrared (far red *) light on plants is not entirely established yet, but we do know from the plant scientists in the USDA that it can inhibit germination and growth in some plants. Infrared light can *reverse* the action started by red light, i.e., germination; the two kinds, red and infrared, can be applied alternately to a plant, each will reverse the other's action, and the last kind applied will govern.

Ultraviolet radiation (invisible; sometimes called black light) such as that produced by germicidal or bactericidal lamps, is

* In Europe this is referred to as near infrared.

generally harmful to plants. This light destroys not only bacteria but most other organisms, too. People are benefited by a certain amount of ultraviolet light, which they get from the sun or from lamps, but the same cannot be said of plants. This was learned by a relative of mine who luxuriated in a sunbath every morning and then turned the sunlamp on a shelf of house plants for thirty minutes, with disastrous effect.

ARTIFICIAL LIGHT

Man can produce light of similar quality to that radiated by the sun. He can deliver it in neat glass packages of various sizes and shapes of tubes or bulbs, called lamps. Artificial light can either supplement or replace sunlight for many purposes. Artificial light can be controlled in its quantity, quality and duration. Our ability to maneuver and control artificial light makes it possible to grow ornamental plants (and food plants, too, although they are not the subject of this book) in our homes, at any time of the year, in a sunless interior.

All living things absorb light from the sun according to their needs. The light required by plants is different than the light required by man or by fish. It may seem unnecessary, perhaps even undesirable, to duplicate the sun's complete spectrum in an artificial lamp that is to be used to aid plant growth. We do not, therefore, need to search for a fluorescent lamp that exactly simulates the sun's light. Instead of an incandescent illuminator which is a small edition of our fiery sun, the cool, gentle light of fluorescent lamps has been proved a reliable light source for growing plants indoors.

WHITE FLUORESCENT LAMPS

The names that manufacturers give to their fluorescent lamps are not to be taken literally. A "daylight" lamp does not really simulate daylight; a "natural white" lamp does not actually duplicate the sun's light; a "cool white" lamp feels no different to the touch than a "warm white" lamp.

The special-purpose fluorescent lamps, producing light that is called red, blue, gold, pink, green, etc., can be ignored as being either inefficient or unsuitable for plant growth. They have been tried, tested, and experimented with, and proven to be of little or no value in a fluorescent light garden.

It is from the shades of "white" fluorescent lamps (remember, the sun's light is white, being a combination of all the colors of the rainbow) that we should select our artificial light source for growing plants.

There are at least eight shades of white fluorescent lamps on the market today. The three main lamp manufacturers, General Electric, Sylvania, and Westinghouse, manufacture almost all of the shades, in almost all of the sizes and types of lamps described in Chapter 3.

The various shades of white fluorescent light are produced by using different proportions of fluorescent powders, or phosphors, to coat the inside of a fluorescent tube. The lamps all emit a white light, and they all produce a high level of yellow/green radiation (because fluorescent lamps are, first of all, designed for the purpose of aiding human vision), but one lamp may be high in blue and deficient in red radiation, or vice versa, and so on.

Some of the names used for white fluorescent lamps are cool white, deluxe cool white, warm white, deluxe warm white,

white, soft white, daylight, and natural white. Many dozens of types and sizes of lamps are made in these colors. Trying to select lamps from a manufacturer's availability chart is an exercise in theory but it is not a very practical way for the amateur to get what he wants or needs for indoor gardening. Lamp manufacturers do not sell directly to the consumer and no dealer can stock every color of lamp in every type and size. I learned quite a few years ago to select my lamps for horticultural use from those usually carried in stock by local dealers, except when I needed enough lamps at one time to obligate myself to taking a full case, which most dealers will order for a customer.

The lamps that are usually available at a hardware store or a retail electrical supply house are cool white, daylight, warm white, and natural white, the last offered only by Sylvania. Table IV shows the color quality, in general terms, of the light produced by lamps bearing these designations.

TABLE IV.

RELATIVE QUANTITIES OF LIGHT EMITTED BY WHITE FLUORESCENT LAMPS

Name of lamp	violet/blue (needed by plants)	green/yellow (not needed by plants)	orange/red (needed by plants)
Cool white	good	excellent	good
Daylight	excellent	very good	deficient
Warm white	deficient	good	very good
Natural white	deficient	good	excellent

Fortunately, theory and practice parallel one another: when I use white fluorescent lamps, my best growing and flowering results are obtained from a one-to-one combination of daylight and natural lamps; second best from a one-to-one combination of daylight and warm white lamps; and third best from cool white lamps alone.

PLANT GROWTH LAMPS

Two manufacturers make lamps that have been engineered and designed for the sole purpose of aiding plant growth. The lamps are trade marked "Gro-Lux," made by Sylvania Lighting Products; and "Plant-Gro," manufactured by Westinghouse Electric Corporation. These plant growth lamps are actually modifications of white fluorescent lamps, inasmuch as they emit the same rays as the other white lamps: violet/blue, green/yellow, and orange/red. However, the plant growth lamps have a relatively low output of green/yellow light and high levels of blue and red light, and consequently the light they emit appears lavender to the human eye. Enough green/yellow light is produced by these lamps to enable one to see and tend his plants, but use of such lamps for reading or sewing might result in severe eyestrain.

Gro-Lux and Plant-Gro lamps are similar, but not identical. This is obvious to the eye when the two are used side by side. The Gro-Lux lamp appears to have a little more blue and a little less green/yellow than the Plant-Gro lamp, and thus gives a more lavender light.

Gro-Lux lamps are available in preheat, rapid start, and instant start types, and in eight different wattages and sizes, including two circlines. There is also one Gro-Lux lamp of the high output type and three of the very high output type. The latter are useful for growing commercial vegetable crops and the flowering plants such as chrysanthemums that have high energy requirements. Sylvania Lighting Products conducts a continuous research program to develop newer and better light sources for horticultural use.

Plant-Gro lamps are available in 15-, 20- and 40-watt sizes.

Both brands of plant growth lamps are the equivalent of other standard fluorescent lamps in electrical and physical characteristics and operate in the same fixtures that take standard fluorescent lamps of the same wattage rating.

Although Gro-Lux lamps have been available since 1961, and Plant-Gro since 1962, you are not likely to find them at the hardware store unless you make arrangements with the owner to stock them for you. Garden centers and retail electrical supply houses are beginning to stock Gro-Lux lamps, and several of the mail-order equipment dealers listed in the *Where to Buy* section of this book handle either or both brands of plant growth lamps. If you are unable to find the lamps locally or by mail, write to the manufacturer requesting the name and address of the dealer nearest you. For Gro-Lux information, write to Sylvania Lighting Products, 60 Boston Street, Salem, Massachusetts. For information about where to buy Plant-Gro lamps, write to Westinghouse Lamp Division, Westinghouse Electric Corporation, Bloomfield, New Jersey.

Using plant growth lamps

I use many plant growth lamps in my various fluorescent light gardens throughout the house. Numerous generations of many, many kinds of plants have been raised in my gardens since experimental models of Gro-Lux lamps were tested in my home before such lamps appeared on the market.

I use Gro-Lux lamps for all methods of plant propagation—germination of seeds, rooting of cuttings, etc.; to start tubers into growth; and for all young plants. In fact, I use Gro-Lux lamps almost exclusively throughout my indoor gardens, only occasionally mixing them with cool white or daylight lamps.

Many of my gardening friends and I experienced a situation with Gro-Lux lamps that I hope you will be able to avoid. We found that some plants—notably African violets, gloxinias and other gesneriads, and begonias—are stimulated extraordinarily by Gro-Lux lamps. The plants seemed to grow and mature too quickly, and looked as if they were exhausted. Mistakenly, I concluded that the lamps were at fault, and I began to mix my light sources, one Gro-Lux lamp to one cool white or daylight tube. The puzzle was solved when a trenchant friend said, "Give those plants more fertilizer, silly!" This seemed altogether too simple an answer to what I thought was a complicated problem. But it is the right answer. Plant growth lamps produce almost ideal light for ornamental plants, and the other factors of culture and environment must be close to ideal, too.

When changing from conventional white fluorescent lamps to Gro-Lux or Plant-Gro lamps, increase the distance between tops of plants and tubes by about half, at first, and gradually bring the lamps closer to the plants over a period of, say, ten days to two weeks. Otherwise, the plants may be shocked by the abrupt increase in effective light intensity, and take several weeks to recover from the setback.

From plant growth lamps you get back in radiant energy usable by plants nearly 100 per cent of the electrical power you put into the lamp. From conventional white fluorescent lamps you realize in usable radiation about 50 per cent of the power you pay for—the balance goes into radiation that plants do not need or use.

Appearance of plants under plant growth lamps

A flowering plant, say an African violet, moved from a window sill or from under the illumination from conventional fluorescent lights and placed under Gro-Lux or Plant-Gro lamps changes its visual appearance instantly and dramatically. Every bit of flower color is enhanced and the foliage looks lush and vibrant and exceedingly healthy. When plant growth lamps were introduced, no small number of growers seemed to feel a little guilty about using them, not because of the cultural effect of the lamps on the growth of the plants but because of the appearance of the plants. They felt it might be slightly dishonest to make plants look as beautiful as they appear under plant growth lamps. This argument is undoubtedly valid when applied to plants displayed for sale: an uninformed buyer might feel that he had been misled when he takes his plant home and discovers that it looks quite ordinary in natural light. But my conscience has never been bothered the least bit by the enhanced beauty of my plants under plant growth lamps, any more than it is bothered by my personal use of cosmetics. I accept the enriched appearance of the plants as an unadvertised dividend from the lamps.

You will probably notice a difference in the appearance of your own skin when your hands and arms are lighted by plant growth lamps as you tend your plants—you will look very healthy up to your elbows. And should you wonder if someone really *does,* just maneuver her head into the path of light from a plant growth lamp. You *and* her hairdresser will know for sure!

INCANDESCENT LIGHT

From 75 to 85 per cent of the power consumed by an incandescent lamp is dissipated as heat through infrared radiation. Most field crops (vegetables) are high energy growing plants that require more far red (infrared) radiation for normal development than would be provided by fluorescent lamps.

When these plants are grown indoors without sunlight, up to 20 per cent of the total radiation (measured by wattage) should be in incandescent lamps.

Most house plants, however, grew naturally in shaded woods or jungles, and are low energy growing plants that do not require much infrared light. The low level of infrared radiation that is provided by fluorescent lamps seems sufficient for them.

If you cannot allay the feeling that you ought to have an incandescent bulb here and there in your fluorescent light garden, go ahead and use them. The infrared light they emit will do no more harm than it does good. An incandescent lamp can burn plants, however, so it must be located at a considerably greater distance from the plants than a fluorescent lamp. The heat radiated by an incandescent bulb can increase the temperature of the air around the plants to an unfavorable degree, requiring extra care in ventilation and temperature control. And the most cogent argument against using incandescent bulbs in an indoor garden is an economic one. You get back in the form of visible light only 15 to 25 per cent of the power you put into the lamp. The rest is money wasted in producing unwanted heat.

As you know from household accidents, it is dangerous to splash water on a hot incandescent bulb—the bulb may explode into flying fragments of glass. There is always the possibility of splashing water on a lighted lamp in an artificial light garden. Cold water does not damage a fluorescent lamp. However, I recommend that any incandescent bulbs used be made of glass that resists thermal shock. For example, use a 40-watt oven lamp instead of a conventional 40-watt bulb, or use bulbs made to perform in outdoor conditions of rain and snow.

I have not been able to prove to myself that plants grown in my home need any light other than fluorescent illumination.

None of my flourescent light gardens are equipped for incandescent bulbs.

SUMMARY OF LAMPS

After years of experience during which I have tried almost every color of fluorescent lamp available, with hundreds of *kinds* of plants, in an ordinary household environment, I know that any of the available shades of white fluorescent light may be used successfully provided other environmental and cultural factors are supplied according to a plant's needs. Some lamps are better than others, but plants will grow and flower under any of the lamps.

My own preferences are: (1) Gro-Lux lamps; (2) a combination of Gro-Lux lamps and either daylight or cool white lamps, one of each or two growth lamps to one white lamp; (3) daylight and natural lamps, one to one; (4) daylight and warm white lamps, one to one; (5) cool white lamps.

DURATION OF LIGHT

Our knowledge of photoperiodism, or the response of plants to the relative lengths of periods of darkness and light, is scant when compared to the vast numbers of kinds of plants that exist on this earth.

Although we know that plants fall into the four categories listed earlier in this chapter, we do not always know which plant falls into which category. The failure of a plant to flower in a fluorescent light garden, when its other cultural requirements are being met, may be due to dark periods of incorrect length.

Fortunately for indoor gardeners, most house plants fall in the *indeterminate* or *daylength-neutral* category: they will flower and fruit (set seed) under a wide range of day lengths and do not demand precise timing of their dark periods, just so they get some darkness in every 24-hour period.

In my plant factory, the lights are on for 16 hours, from 7 A.M. to 11 P.M., every day of the year, controlled by a timer. In the fluorescent gardens that are scattered around the house, the lights burn a minimum of 12 hours a day, and may burn as long as 18 hours. They are turned on at 7 A.M. and turned off whenever my day ends.

There is no rule that says your fluorescent garden lamps must be turned on during daylight hours and off at night. The timing can be completely reversed, with the lights on during the night and off during the day, as long as the dark period can be really dark. I have not tried it, but I do not think this reverse timing would work so well in a room flooded with natural light from the outside during the period that is supposed to be night for the plants. This reverse timing procedure is frequently used by commercial growers to spread the demand load on their power supply—half of their plants are irradiated at night and half in the daytime.

Exceptions to the daylength-neutral category among house plants that have come to my attention are mentioned in Part III of this book.

If you do not have a timer to control your lights, and you know that you will not be at home to turn the lights on and off during a given 24-hour period, leave the lights off altogether for that period rather than letting them burn around the clock. Plants must have a period of darkness in each 24 hours. They will not suffer much from missing one day's light, but their growth process can be upset radically if they miss a dark period.

COST OF FLUORESCENT ILLUMINATION

The cost of operating electrical equipment varies, depending on the rates charged by the local power company. In my locality, the average cost per kilowatt hour in the home is just under three cents. Two 40-watt lamps plus a 20-watt ballast equals 100 watts. 100 watts burned for 16 hours a day equals 1600 watt hours, or 1.6 kilowatt hours, or about five cents for a 16-hour day for two 40-watt lamps.

Power companies have step rates, whereby the more power you consume in a given period, the lower the cost per kilowatt hour.

MEASURING FLUORESCENT ILLUMINATION

Various authors, not including this one, recommend the minimum, maximum, or optimum light level for growing different plants indoors under fluorescent lamps in terms, usually, of footcandles. The footcandle is a measure of the intensity of light. The engineering definition is: the footcandle is the normal incident illumination produced by unit candle power at a distance of one foot. It is virtually impossible to produce accurately a light intensity of one footcandle except in a laboratory, but if you would like to see the approximate intensity of one footcandle, strike a paper match in a completely dark room. After the initial flare has died down, hold the match about four inches above some flat surface—the surface will then be illuminated to the extent of about one footcandle. To see 400 footcandles, hold a 100-watt, inside frosted incandescent bulb base up about $4\frac{1}{2}$ inches above a surface, in an otherwise completely darkened room. The surface will be illuminated roughly to the extent of 400 footcandles directly under the bulb.

Outdoor illumination varies from 10,000 footcandles at high noon on a completely cloudless June 21st, down to 900 footcandles on a completely overcast December 21st at high noon. Window sill footcandles may vary from a high of 8,000 on a southern exposure on June 21 to a low of 200 on a northern exposure on a cloudy day in December.

The table of illumination in footcandles cannot be taken literally but it will give you some idea of the light values to be expected from fluorescent tubes at various distances from plants. Table V was worked out for 40-watt tubes, but can apply to the center of any T-12 (tubular, 1½″ diameter) type of tube.

Light meters are available for the measurement of fluorescent light in footcandles, ranging in price from about thirty to five hundred dollars. There is as yet no light meter available that will measure accurately the effective energy units of Gro-Lux and Plant-Gro lamps.

If the cost of a light meter is too much for you, and it certainly is for me, there are other ways to measure light in footcandles.

Every student knows that he can virtually double the light which falls on his desk if he removes the 50-watt incandescent bulb from his reading lamp and replaces it with a 100-watt bulb. However, if we replace a 20-watt fluorescent tube over a table full of growing plants with a 40-watt fluorescent tube, the same doubling of illumination does not take place, except for plants located at the extreme ends of the table. A plant located under the center of the 40-watt fluorescent tube will receive scarcely any more light than it did under the center of the 20-watt fluorescent tube.

TABLE V.

TABLE OF ILLUMINATION IN FOOTCANDLES AT VARIOUS DISTANCES FROM
TWO OR FOUR 40-WATT STANDARD COOL-WHITE FLUORESCENT
LAMPS MOUNTED APPROXIMATELY 2 INCHES FROM A
WHITE-PAINTED REFLECTING SURFACE.***

		Illumination	
Distance from lamps	Two lamps * Used **	Four lamps *	
		Used **	New
(inches)	(fc)	(fc)	(fc)
1	1,100	1,600	1,800
2	860	1,400	1,600
3	680	1,300	1,400
4	570	1,100	1,300
5	500	940	1,150
6	420	820	1,000
7	360	720	900
8	330	660	830
9	300	600	780
10	280	560	720
11	260	510	660
12	240	480	600
18	130	320	420
24	100	190	260

* Center to center distance between the lamps was 2 inches.
** These lamps had been used for approximately 200 hours.
*** Table developed by the USDA, Beltsville, Maryland.

The explanation for this state of affairs lies in the brightness per unit area of the incandescent bulb and the fluorescent tube, respectively. The 100-watt incandescent bulb is no larger than the 50-watt incandescent bulb but it produces twice as much light from the same luminous area. A square inch of the glass envelope of a 100-watt incandescent bulb is twice as bright (i.e., emits twice as much light) as a square inch of the glass surface of a 50-watt incandescent bulb.

On the other hand, a 2-inch long section in the center of a 40-watt fluorescent tube produces no more light than a 2-inch long section in the center of a 20-watt fluorescent tube. The 40-watt fluorescent tube gives roughly twice as much *total illumination* as a 20-watt fluorescent tube *because it is twice as long,* but inch for inch it is no brighter.

We learned in elementary physics classes in school that a point source of light follows *the inverse square law.* The intensity of the light decreases with the square of the distance from the point source. A book page in a dark room 6 feet from a single burning candle will not receive one-half as much light as a book held 3 feet from that same candle. It will receive only one-fourth as much light because the candle flame is more or less a point source of light.

Compared to a 4-foot long fluorescent tube, an incandescent bulb is virtually a point source of light. Consequently, an incandescent lamp closely follows the inverse square law. The soft, diffused light from a fluorescent tube, on the other hand, does not diminish so markedly if the distance from tube to plants is doubled.

If we want to measure the light from fluorescent fixtures, therefore, we cannot rely on the watt-rating of the tubes nor on the photometric law that illumination decreases with the square of the distance. How, then, shall we measure the light which falls on our plants from an overhead fluorescent light fixture? How can we determine the height above our plants at which to suspend the fluorescent tubes to produce the light level that is recommended for growing particular plants?

Measuring light in footcandles

A light-measuring device suitable for measuring footcandles must be one that is pointed toward the source of light in order to measure the amount of light being received.

If a photographic exposure meter is to be used for direct measurement of light in footcandles it must of necessity be capable of measuring incident light. Most photographic exposure meters, however, are reflected-light meters. Instead of being pointed toward the source of light to measure the oncoming light, they are aimed at the scene or object to be photographed. Such instruments measure the light reflected from the scene and are commonly calibrated in candles per square foot.

The indoor gardener who possesses a photographic exposure meter of the incident light type can use it for direct measurement of plant illumination under fluorescent tubes by holding the meter in the plant area and pointing it toward the fluorescent fixture. The instruction book that came with the exposure meter will tell him how to convert the meter reading to footcandles in case his instrument is not calibrated to read in such units.

Photographic exposure meters of the more popular type, which measure scene brightness rather than incident light, can be used in a makeshift manner to obtain footcandle measurements of reasonable accuracy. The method employed is similar to the "white card" method used for determining the correct photographic exposure for copying a picture or document.

The area under the fluorescent fixture to be measured for illumination level is covered with a clean white sheet or a large piece of pure white (photographic quality) blotting paper. Wrapping paper, shelf-lining paper, even writing paper may be used if it is pure white and enough thicknesses are used to insure maximum reflectance. This white reflecting layer must be at the level of the plant leaves, not at the surface of the table where the pots will rest.

With the white reflecting surface in place, set the photographic exposure meter for ASA 10 film speed. The meter is pointed at the white surface at a distance away no greater than the narrowest dimension of the white card or sheet. For example, if a 30 x 40-inch photographic blotter is used, the exposure meter should be held not more than 30 inches away from the center of the blotter. Exposure settings indicated by the photographic exposure meter under these conditions can be converted into footcandles by use of Table VI.

TABLE VI.
CONVERSION OF PHOTOGRAPHIC EXPOSURE METER SETTINGS
INTO FOOTCANDLES

Meter Reading		Footcandles
1/100th second	1/60th second	
f. 3.5	f. 4.5	400
f. 4	f. 5	500
f. 4.5	f. 5.6	650
f. 5	f. 6.3	800
f. 5.6	f. 7	1000
f. 6.3	f. 8	1300
f. 7	f. 9	1600
f. 8	f. 10	2000
f. 9	f. 11	2400
f. 10	f. 12.7	3200
f. 11	f. 14	4000
f. 12.7	f. 16	5200
f. 14	f. 18	6400

The accuracy of footcandle measurements

Even though a thirty dollar photoelectric exposure meter is used to measure the light from fluorescent tubes, the resulting values will be only approximately correct. There are several reasons for the inaccuracy. Good quality photographic exposure meters of the same manufacturer may give indications within the range 500 to 800 footcandles for the same illumination condition. Mechanical injury to an exposure meter can further increase the discrepancy, producing lower than normal readings. Age and the effects of heat on the photoelectric cell are bound to reduce the efficiency of a meter, resulting in discrepant readings. These sources of inaccuracy are further influenced by the manner in which the plant grower handles the meter. Casting too much of a shadow on the white surface while taking reflected light readings will introduce an error. Inaccuracies in aiming the reflected-light meter at the white surface or the incident-light meter at the light source will also affect the footcandle measurement.

Color differences both in the sensitivity of photoelectric exposure meters and in the light emission characteristics of different kinds of fluorescent tubes are additional complexities affecting footcandle measurements. Most photographic exposure meters have selenium cells as their light-sensitive element. The selenium cells respond to light in much the same fashion as the human eye. Recently there has appeared on the market a type of battery-powered photographic exposure meter which employs a cadmium sulphide photocell. The latter variety of light-sensitive element is particularly responsive to invisible light at both ends of the solar spectrum.

Obviously, a selenium cell light meter and a cadmium sulphide cell light meter, calibrated to give the same footcandle reading under daylight fluorescent light, will give markedly dissimilar readings when used under Gro-Lux or Plant-Gro lamps which have a deficiency in the yellow range of light waves to which the selenium cells are most responsive.

What good are light meters?

If two brand new meters can give readings as far apart as 500 and 800 footcandles for the same light situation, and this error can be multiplied by the age and condition of the meter or the manner of using it, one might seriously question the utility of photographic exposure meters to the indoor gardener. The indoor gardener who owns an incident-light photographic exposure meter will find it useful nevertheless. Although it may not give absolute values for illumination levels, it will provide very useful information about relative illumination in his plant growing area.

Let us assume that plants are being grown successfully under fluorescent lights at a certain distance and you want to enlarge the growing area by putting in additional fluorescent fixtures suspended farther away from the plants. A reading of the present setup will give a value representing "satisfactory illumination for plant growth." The meter can then be used under the new light setup to determine, by trial and error movement of the fixtures, the location that will give the same "satisfactory illumination for plant growth." It does not matter if this condition is represented by the number 300, or 590, or 900 on your exposure meter dial, you will be able to duplicate the desired level through use of the light meter.

In the same fashion, a light meter will give reasonably accurate indications of the relative amount of light received at the ends, sides, and center of a growing space under a fluorescent light unit or the relative increase and decrease in light level as a unit is lowered and raised above the plants, and relative decrease as lamps age.

Changing from white to Gro-Lux lamps

The light from Gro-Lux lamps deceives the selenium cell light meter in the same way that it deceives the human eye. This happens because neither the eye nor the photocell is particularly sensitive to short wavelength violet and long wavelength red light, the invisible rays. If Gro-Lux lamps replace cool white lamps in a fluorescent tube fixture for plant growth, a meter reading using a selenium photocell will show a reduction in footcandles. Actually, the amount of light useful in plant growth will have been increased considerably by the change from cool white to Gro-Lux lamps.

It is possible, by mathematical calculation, to convert footcandle measurements to absolute energy units that will be useful in calibrating Gro-Lux lighting conditions. A method has been published by C. J. Bernier of Sylvania Lighting Products, and reprints are available from that firm at Danvers, Massachusetts.

However, the house-plant grower who has forgotten how to manipulate a slide rule will be better advised to rely on biology rather than mathematics to calibrate his fluorescent light setup. The plants are the most reliable indicators of artificial light conditions which suit their needs. Their telltale indications of insufficient light or too much light for optimum growth at a given temperature and relative humidity level are discussed in Part III.

And 'tis my faith, that every flower
Enjoys the air it breathes.
WILLIAM WORDSWORTH

5

Atmosphere

The maintenance of adequate levels of illumination in an indoor garden is but one requirement of successful gardening. Light is important, indeed, and no one would try to grow house plants by candle light. But sometimes gardeners who are well aware of the effect of both quality and quantity of fluorescent light fail to evaluate properly the importance of maintaining correct temperature, humidity, and ventilation for the plants they wish to grow.

TEMPERATURE

Most house plants are comfortable in about the same conditions of temperature and humidity as the people with whom they share a home.

Temperature influences the various plant growth processes— the rate with which roots absorb water, transpiration, respiration, the rate with which plants assimilate carbon dioxide, and the production of chlorophyll. Plants manufacture their food during the hours of light, but they use the food—in other words, they do most of their growing—during the dark period. A night temperature about 10 degrees lower than the daytime temperature aids this growth process.

In our Long Island home, we strive for a night temperature of 60 to 62 degrees, a day temperature of about 72 degrees and not over 75 degrees, and a relative humidity of about 55 per cent. These temperatures are relatively easy to maintain during the winter months, with humidity the principal problem. In summer the daytime temperatures are apt to go out of control in many parts of the United States, with night temperatures failing to drop as they should for best growing conditions.

During one recent summer, the temperature in my plant factory reached 100 degrees a number of times, and not once in almost three months did it get down to the desired 62 degrees at night. A few gloxinias continued to grow and flower in a half-hearted manner, but most of my other plants reacted to the continuing high temperatures by stopping their growing activity. The African violets and other gesneriads, the geraniums, the begonias—all sat in a state of suspended animation. This trance seemed to be a built-in protective device. When the weather finally cooled for a few nights, the plants went right on with what they had been doing when the hot weather inhibited their normal growth routine. Buds that had not budged for weeks opened into flowers, with no bud blast, and the plants continued to produce new buds as if they had not been interrupted. When I noticed that the plants were not growing, I stopped fertilizing and cut the light period from 16 to 12 hours for the plants on one three-decker bench, but continued fertilizing and 16-hour lighting for those on the other set of benches. I noticed no difference in the two groups of miscellaneous plants—both groups started to grow and progressed at the same pace when the period of cool nights resumed.

This worrisome experience convinced me of the importance of a drop in night temperature for most house plants.

Our heating thermostat in the plant room is set at 62 degrees for the winter, and requires resetting for the 72-degree daytime temperature only when a north wind hits the house. Otherwise, the ballasts in the considerable number of fluorescent light fixtures produce enough heat to provide the additional daytime temperature. A smaller installation of fluorescent light fixtures, located in a larger room than ours, probably would not emit enough additional heat when the lamps are on to produce a 10-degree rise over night-time conditions.

A thermometer is an essential indoor gardening accessory. An adequate one can be purchased for less than a dollar. It is not so important to know the temperature to the precise fraction of a degree as it is to be able to check on the variation in temperature.

The temperatures in different parts of a room may vary as much as 10 degrees. Even in a small room, you will probably discover that one particular plant seems to do better in one certain spot on a bench than in any other location in the room. Unless there is radiant heat in the floor, the lower part of the room will be cooler than the upper area, and one corner may be cooler by several degrees than another.

A maximum/minimum thermometer (cost, eight to ten dollars) is a useful instrument in an indoor garden, especially for people who are away from home during the day and unable to check on the conditions in the growing areas several times between morning and night. This instrument records the minimum and maximum temperatures reached during any given period.

RELATIVE HUMIDITY

I wish that relative humidity were understood as well as temperature is, and that humidity control equipment were as readily available and as widely used as temperature equipment.

Relative humidity is a measure of the amount of water vapor present in the air when compared to the total amount which the air can possibly hold at the given temperature. Relative humidity is expressed in *per cent* of saturation, not in degrees on an arbitrary scale.

The warmer the air, the greater the amount of water vapor it can hold. The cooler the air, the less water vapor it can hold. That explains why, in the winter when the indoor air is heated, the relative humidity drops although the absolute amount of water vapor in the air has remained constant. An example: the outdoor temperature is 40 degrees and the outdoor relative humidity is 60 per cent. When this air is brought inside and heated to 72 degrees, the relative humidity falls to approximately 20 per cent. During the winter months in the northern states this is not an unusual situation in many homes and city apartments.

Most porous materials like wood, paper, and fabric have the ability to absorb moisture from the air under conditions of high humidity, and to return this moisture to the air under low humidity conditions. Such materials are said to be hygroscopic. When humidity conditions are such that a certain hygroscopic material is neither receiving nor giving moisture to the air, the material is in hygroscopic balance with the air. The fact that wood and certain kinds of glue are hygroscopic explains why furniture joints dry out and loosen in heated, unhumidified rooms during the winter.

Most house plants prefer a relative humidity of 50 to 60 per cent for normal growth. Moisture in the air greatly restricts the amount of water lost by plants through their leaves. Unless some artificial or mechanical means of increasing the relative humidity in the room during the heating season is provided, most house plants will languish in the desertlike dryness.

So will people, for that matter. Dry air will evaporate moisture from your skin and make you feel chilled. Remember how cool you feel when you come out of the water after a swim on a windy day? The wind evaporates the water off your skin and really cools you. The same thing happens in a heated house or apartment. The dry air evaporates your skin's moisture, and even though the room temperature may be above 70 degrees, you still feel cold. By raising the relative humidity from 20 per cent (which is about average for an unhumidified heated room) to 60 per cent, you can save the expense of heating the room by $4\frac{1}{2}$ degrees. This amounts to about 10 per cent of your fuel bill. Monetary savings aside, you will be more comfortable and healthier.

TABLE VII.
RELATIVE HUMIDITY AND TEMPERATURE FOR COMFORT

If relative humidity is		Temperature for comfort should be
60%		71° F
50%	(ideal)	72° F
40%		73° F
30%		74° F
20%		75–$\frac{1}{2}$° F

A humid atmosphere is essential for plant propagation. Lack of humidity often is responsible for the failure of seeds to sprout or of stem and leaf cuttings of many plants to root.

Unlike thermometers, a reliable humidity indicator (hygrometer) cannot be purchased for a dollar or so. Hygrometers range in price from three to three hundred dollars. It is our experience that a humidity indicator costing under five dollars is a waste of the indoor gardener's money. An instrument on which you can rely will have a sensitive element made from human hair (a hygroscopic material) and it will cost between seven and fifteen dollars. It is a safe guess that during the winter heating season, your home and your indoor garden have a relative humidity which is far too low for either plant or human comfort. A reliable humidity indicator is one of the best investments the serious indoor gardener can make.

Small enclosures can be humidified by setting the plants over a shallow tray filled with moist peat, sand, vermiculite, or gravel. The material in the tray *must* be kept moist. The purpose is to *increase the moist surface area* from which water can be evaporated to maintain moist air around the plants. When the growing area is enclosed with plastic sheeting, with allowance for ventilation, this method is reasonably effective. My own experience, however, causes me to doubt the effectiveness of this system for a small group of plants on a tray in the open air in a room. In spite of all that has been written and recommended about it, this is at best a makeshift method which I have never found to be wholly satisfactory or successful. Misting plant foliage with tepid water several times a day in hot weather increases the effectiveness of such an arrangement, however, and may constitute the difference between success and failure.

In a large indoor garden such as my plant factory, where there are many plants, the system works better. The moist surface of large areas of vermiculite and the transpiration of many plants combine to help in the maintenance of adequate relative humidity in the area.

Plastic sheeting draped over and around a table or bench full of plants is helpful in creating an enclosed area in which the relative humidity can be held at a higher range than is found in the rest of the room. Such an enclosure should not be altogether air tight. The plastic film retains the moisture in the enclosure but does allow a certain amount of air movement and transfer. An indoor garden draped with plastic sheeting is not the most esthetically pleasing sight to behold, but the plastic can be opened or removed when company is expected.

You should be warned that, just as too low a relative humidity in your home will cause damage to furnishings, a consistently high relative humidity brings its problems, too, as residents of any seashore know. Consistent high humidity may damage wallpaper and some household furnishings. In my plant factory, where we maintain a relative humidity of 55 to 60 per cent, we covered the walls completely, from ceiling to floor, with clear plastic sheeting before installing the benches. I regret that we did not cover the ceiling in similar fashion, because moisture condenses on the ceiling. We will have to replace the ceiling tiles if we ever wish to use the space for living quarters again.

There are several mechanical means of increasing the relative humidity, ranging from the crude method of evaporating water by boiling it on a hot plate to the more sophisticated use of a fully automatic humidifier which is attached to the home's plumbing system.

A modified and safer version of the boiling water system is an electric steam vaporizer, satisfactory in an area of up to 1000 to 1200 cubic feet (about 12 x 12 x 8 feet). Most of these vaporizers shut themselves off when they boil dry, so no harm is done to the device, but you have to be there to refill them. They are readily available at drug or department stores or may be ordered by mail for around ten dollars. I do not like this kind of device because its steam increases the room *temperature* when I do not want or need more heat, and because the power consumed costs about twenty-five cents a day.

The most satisfactory device we have found is a portable *cool-vapor* humidifier which costs about thirty dollars. It produces a fog of cool-water vapor by means of mechanical water breakers and blowers, handles an area of about 20 x 20 x 8 feet, and costs about five cents a day to operate. It holds about two gallons of water and will operate a full 24 hours, if necessary, before refilling. Two brands are Hankscraft and Oster. Department stores usually stock cool-vapor humidifiers with their small appliances, and the machines are listed in Montgomery Ward and Sears Roebuck mail-order catalogs.

A table fountain with a recirculating pump can be set among plants on a fluorescent lighted table or bench. The rise and fall of water from the fountain adds moisture to the air around the plants. A fountain adds a touch of natural beauty and makes a warm room *seem* cooler. I have several small fountains on my plant benches, but confess that they are not always in operation. I love the music of running water outdoors, but indoors the sound of trickling, splashing, and dripping water makes me vaguely uneasy—somehow I always assume that somewhere the plumbing has sprung a leak.

A humidistat connected to a humidifying device turns the machine on and off, much the same way that a thermostat controls the heating or cooling equipment in the home. A humidistat is a precision instrument, costing between fifteen and twenty dollars. We have found it of great value in our own situation, where no one is at home during the day to check the plant room occasionally. Our humidistat normally is set to turn the cool-vapor humidifier on when the relative humidity drops just below 55 per cent, and off when it reaches 60 per cent. An oil burner supply store is probably the best place to buy a humidistat.

The kind of automatic humidistat that is sold for about ten dollars as an accessory for *de*humidifiers is not suitable for controlling a humidifier.

During the summer in many parts of this country the problem is one of too high a relative humidity. Do not worry about high humidity unless you see evidence of mildew or fungus. These undesirable growths can be prevented with proper sanitation, spacing of plants, ventilation, and spraying. Extremely high humidity is not desirable, but will not harm plants as low humidity does.

VENTILATION

Ventilation—the circulation of fresh air—is important in preventing the development of disease organisms. Plants continuously lose water through their leaves in a process known as transpiration. Poor ventilation allows this water vapor to condense on the leaf surface, offering ideal germination conditions for the spores of disease-producing organisms. Ventilation allows for the entrance of carbon dioxide necessary for photosynthesis and also provides a good supply of oxygen for respiration.

There are some *air-borne* substances that harm plants. The slightest waft of manufactured gas around plants will cause foliage to yellow and buds to blacken and drop. Natural gas (butane) and "bottled" or propane gas (a liquefied petroleum gas) seem to be not at all noxious to plants. If you suspect leaking gas, place a tomato plant in the area. If gas is present, the tomato plant will droop, the leaves will curl down and discolor.

Gasoline engines and some manufacturing and industrial processes produce fumes noxious to certain plants. I concede, reluctantly, that the presence of air-borne noxious fumes from a factory is a reason not to have an indoor garden.

When the indoor plant collection keeps increasing in size and in number, as it inevitably does in a fluorescent light garden, there is a tendency to crowd plants to make room for just a few more. Ideally, plants should be spaced so they do not touch, to allow the proper air circulation around pot and plant.

A 36-inch exhaust fan in our attic is controlled by a thermostat located in the plant factory. During the summer, the thermostat turns the fan on when the temperature in the plant room reaches 75 degrees, and off at 70 degrees. The benches have "half-walls" of plastic sheeting, so the draft created by the fan's pulling air through the window does not hit the plants directly. Of course, the fan does not reduce the temperature of the air, because during the daytime it pulls in hot air from out of doors, but by keeping the air circulating gently there seems to be a good chance that leaf temperatures are kept a little lower than they would be without the circulation. When the outside temperature falls slightly on summer evenings, the exhaust fan gives the plants the benefit of the cooling long before natural air movement would be effective. This excellent ventilation does a lot to counteract the extreme heat mentioned earlier.

AIR CONDITIONING

People are inclined to think of an air conditioning machine only as a cooling device, which of course it is. Actually, it is more than that. It does what its name implies: conditions the air, which includes not only controlling the temperature but also the relative humidity in the enclosed area in which the machine operates.

Provided plants are not fanned by a draft from the air conditioning unit, they should be quite safe and comfortable in an air conditioned room in which you are comfortable.

I would question the advisability of installing cooling equipment solely for the sake of the plants. I know of a huge range of greenhouses in which more than a million dollars was spent to install air cooling equipment. The people in the greenhouses enjoy ideal comfort, but the leaf temperature of the plants has not been reduced.

My plant factory is not cooled mechanically, but the air is conditioned by good ventilation. Other parts of our home are cooled mechanically in the hot weather, and the air is humidified mechanically during the winter heating season. The cooling and humidifying equipment was installed, I hasten to add, for the comfort of the people in the house, especially for the one with sensitive sinuses, and not for the benefit of the plants. That the plants thrive in the controlled climate is one more proof that most house plants do well in the same conditions that are enjoyed by the people who grow them.

SUMMARY

The biggest problems to overcome in a fluorescent lighted garden in a home seem to be ventilation in summer and low humidity in winter. Take care of these two, and the temperature will probably take care of itself.

In my plant factory, each bench has its own humidity indicator and maximum/minimum thermometer. I can tell more about the condition of my plants by glancing at these instruments every morning and evening than I can by looking at the plants themselves, because the instruments respond instantaneously to changing conditions, and adverse conditions can be corrected before plants suffer. For example, the vermiculite in one of the benches dries out faster than that in any of the others, because of air currents. A glance at the humidity indicator hanging over that bench warns me that it is time to wet down the vermiculite at once.

6

Culture

THE POTTING MEDIUM

The medium in which a potted plant grows performs two services. It supports the plant, and it is the agent through which roots get air, water, and nourishment. Depending on the medium used, nourishment may come from the medium itself, or from fertilizers that are added to the medium, or from both.

Garden soil is probably the most universally used potting medium. Basically there are two types of soil, inorganic and organic. Inorganic soils are composed mostly of gravel, sand, silt, and clay. Organic soils are sawdust, leaf mold, fern roots, moss, peat, and muck, the last being well-decomposed peat with little or no fibrous structure.

Clay soils are heavy and hold moisture for a long time, and must be loosened by adding sand and organic matter to permit air to enter the soil and to provide drainage.

Loam is a mixture of clay, silt, and sand—silty clay, sandy loam, etc. Loam usually has organic matter present in the form of decayed animal and plant materials.

Materials gathered out of doors and brought inside for

potting should be pasteurized. There are some rugged individualists who maintain that if their soil is good enough for their outdoor gardens, it is quite good enough for potted plants. Perhaps it is, but out of doors Nature handles the balances among diseases, insects, and weed seeds. Indoors, the gardener can more conveniently, easily, and surely deal with these plant enemies by pasteurizing the soil. Garden writers used to admonish us to "sterilize" the soil to be used for potted plants. Sterilizing kills all organisms, desirable and undesirable, and these writers probably meant to tell us to pasteurize the soil.

A small quantity of soil or soil mixture can be pasteurized at home by baking it in the kitchen oven. Wet the material thoroughly and bake it for about 30 minutes at 180 degrees F. Dry material can be pasteurized in the same way, but it takes longer because the air present in dry soil insulates the material against the heat, which is what does the job.

To sterilize soil, killing *all* organisms good and bad, bake it in the oven for 30 minutes at 212 degrees F., which is the boiling point of water. The soil should be thoroughly wet, with water standing on top. Sterilizing is also accomplished by cooking the soil in a pressure cooker for 15 minutes at 15 pounds of pressure, with water in the bottom of the pan.

I do not think home pasteurizing is less expensive than buying a pre-pasteurized potting mix at the garden center. The cost of the gas or electricity to bake the stuff may not amount to much, and perhaps you have the time to clean up the mess and air out the kitchen to get rid of the smell of baked angleworms, but the number of meals you and your family will eat in restaurants for several days while the odor of the baked soil permeates the premises will put this operation on the red side of the ledger.

There are as many soil-mixture recipes for house plants as there are indoor gardeners. Different plants benefit by different basic constituents, but the various soil constituents offer an almost limitless freedom of composition to the soil-mix virtuoso, and plants manage to survive in most of the concoctions.

My own feeling about this subject is that it should not be as complicated and mysterious as a lot of gardeners make it. A potting medium should hold the plant upright in the pot, drain well but retain moisture at the same time, and act as a commissary for the water, air, and nutrition needed by the plant.

I use the same potting mixture for all of the plants in my fluorescent light gardens except epiphytes (air plants) and some cacti and succulents. Heresy this may be, but for me it works, because I fertilize the plants according to their requirements.

My house-plant mixture consists of equal parts by volume of *sphagnum* peat, clean sharp builder's sand, medium perlite, horticultural vermiculite, and a purchased pasteurized potting soil. I buy the perlite, vermiculite, and potting soil at a garden center, usually in bags holding 4 cubic feet. I get my sand by taking empty galvanized containers, such as garbage cans or pails, to a sand and gravel yard where an attendant fills them with sand for a nominal charge. Occasionally I buy sand from a lumber dealer. Sand used for horticultural purposes should be builder's sand, not beach sand. The salt in beach sand is toxic to plants, and no amount of washing or processing the sand seems to remove all the salt. The sphagnum peat is bought in bale size at the garden center; or when I can get it, I use the compressed German horticultural peat which expands when moistened.

The ingredients are mixed in a square 10-gallon, galvanized washtub and used as needed. The sphagnum peat goes in the tub first—it must be moistened by kneading water into it; then the sand, perlite, vermiculite, mixed well after each addition, and last the pasteurized potting soil for bacterial action. I try to be neat about this mixing task, but I usually get in up to my elbows before I am satisfied that the batch is thoroughly mixed. Ah well, as someone has said before, it isn't a green thumb that marks the good gardener, it's a dirty, busy thumb. Dirty hands are an honorable trademark of our avocation.

The potting mixture described is porous and light, and allows root freedom. It provides little nutrients to the plant, and requires a good fertilizing schedule.

Soilless mixtures

Obtaining good top soil for pot plant culture is an ever-increasing problem for the indoor gardener. Although small quantities of many types of soil are available from local florists and garden centers, the nutrient content and physical properties such as aeration and compaction of the diverse packaged soils may sometimes be questioned.

Likewise, in some parts of the country, especially the East, the availability of sand of the proper kind and size is as much of a problem as finding good top soil.

The Department of Floriculture and Ornamental Horticulture, Cornell University, Ithaca, New York, worked for several years to develop a substitute for soil-and-sand mixtures. The Cornell "peat-lite" mixes derived from these studies are light in weight, utilize ingredients readily available, the ingredients used are fairly uniform from one supplier to another, and the mixture is ready for use without being pasteurized.

The nutrient levels of the Cornell mixes are low, so it is necessary that nutrients be added before planting. The addition of 5-10-15 fertilizer to the formula provides nutrients to carry the plants for approximately one to two weeks. After that

TABLE VIII.
CORNELL PEAT-LITE POTTING MIXES

(for one peck)

Mix A

Vermiculite (#2 Terralite)	4 quarts, dry measure
Shredded peat moss (German or Canadian)	4 quarts, dry measure
5-10-15 fertilizer	1 level tablespoonful
Ground limestone	1 level tablespoonful

Mix B

Substitute horticultural grade perlite for the vermiculite. All other ingredients are the same.

period, a regular liquid (water-soluble) fertilizing program should be followed.

The ingredients in a Cornell peat-lite mix must be mixed uniformly. When the mix is used for sowing seeds or transplanting young plants, it must be thoroughly wetted with water. After the initial wetting, wait 30 minutes or overnight and then thoroughly wet the medium again, sow seeds or plant seedlings, and thereafter water as needed. When shifting plants to larger pots, the wetting can be done after plants are repotted.

If the peat moss or vermiculite used for the Cornell mix are excessively dry, it may take several days for the moisture to saturate the medium completely. Take care that plants do not suffer from lack of water during this time. The Cornell mixes have excellent porosity and can be watered heavily without fear of overwatering during a plant's active growing period. Care must be exercised, however, not to oversaturate the medium when plants are not in active growth. Pots containing a peat-lite mix should never be allowed to stand in a saucer of water that would keep the medium too wet.

Excellent results have been obtained with the Cornell mixes in the growing of diverse plants—annuals, geraniums, chrysanthemums, foliage plants, African violets, gloxinias, begonias, and other flowering plants.

The Agricultural Department of the Nassau County (New York) Extension Service publishes a formula for a soilless mix that has been found to be highly satisfactory for house plants, as long as a consistent fertilizing program is followed.

TABLE IX.
1-1-1 POTTING MIX

Ingredient	To prepare a cubic yard (29 cubic feet, or 22 bushels)	To prepare 3 bushels (3-3/4 cubic feet)
Horticultural peat moss	7 bushels	1 bushel
Horticultural perlite	7 bushels	1 bushel
Horticultural vermiculite	7 bushels	1 bushel
Agricultural limestone	10 pounds	1½ pounds
8-40-0 (Magnesium Ammonium Phosphate) medium size	10 pounds	1½ pounds
Potassium sulfate	10 ounces	1½ ounces

Many of the members of our Long Island Gloxinia Society have used this soilless mix for more than a year, and the plants they exhibit at meetings are magnificent—sturdy, floriferous, and beautiful. One member cautions, however, that the grower simply *must* be available to water frequently the plants grown in this mix. Like the weather in the tropics, one minute it is soaking wet and the next minute it is dry.

The University of California has for many years advocated various combinations of sand and peat, and U.C. mixes are used successfully by many indoor gardeners. Slow-release fertilizer is added to the U.C. mixes, about 12 pounds per yard of mix.

It is composed of hoof-and-horn or blood meal, potassium sulfate, superphosphate, dolomite lime, calcium carbonate lime, and gypsum.

TABLE X.
UNIVERSITY OF CALIFORNIA POTTING MIXES

Mix A   100% sand or perlite

Mix B   75% sand or perlite
         25% organic materials as peat moss, sawdust, ground bark, etc.

Mix C   50% sand or perlite
         50% organic materials

Mix D   25% sand or perlite
         75% organic materials

Mix E   100% organic materials

"The U.C. System for Producing Healthy Container-Grown Plants," Manual 23, is one dollar per copy from Agricultural Publications, University Hall, University of California, Berkeley 4, California.

Other soilless media

Coarse sphagnum moss is enjoying a revival of interest, especially for plants in hanging containers, and for tuberous-rooted plants. A consistent fertilizing program is a necessity when this medium is used since the moss provides no nutrients whatsoever. Coarse sphagnum moss has the advantage of excellent draining properties and at the same time it is moisture retentive. If accidentally it is allowed to dry out, however, repeated applications of water are required to resaturate it. It also presents a problem in transplanting: how do you get the roots out of the moss without damaging them? I do not attempt to separate roots from moss fibers, but simply lift out the entire contents of pot or basket and transplant the whole thing to the next larger container.

Horticultural vermiculite by itself is an excellent growing medium for fibrous-rooted plants. It, too, offers only trace-element nutrients to a plant and is successful only with regular fertilizing. Most indoor gardeners who use vermiculite as their growing medium fertilize lightly every time they water plants. I like vermiculite for its light weight, porosity, excellent drainage qualities, and moisture retention. Because of its lightweight nature, it is a little shifty and unstable in a pot, and a stream of water might easily dislodge the entire contents. This problem can be solved to some extent by weighting the surface of the vermiculite with small gravel chips.

Summary

A house plant potting medium must be porous, drain well, and be moisture-retentive.

The potting medium may be soilless, in which case fertilizer must be applied consistently.

The potting medium may be or may contain soil. As a well known commercial nurseryman puts it, Nature grows 'em in dirt and that is good enough for him. He is, however, very careful to pasteurize every speck of soil that goes into his greenhouses, and he composts his soil with generous quantities of grass and other organic material for months before he uses it.

When all is said and done, you will probably be quite satisfied with a packaged pasteurized soil or mixture that you can buy from a garden center, in anything from a pound size to a 4 cubic-foot bag. You will not know what these packaged products contain in the way of plant nutrients, but your plants will inform you by their appearance when they need fertilizing.

SOIL pH

People are sometimes confounded by the term "pH." They do not understand what it is or what it can do for or against their plants, so they disregard it and hope it will go away. Like temperature and humidity, the maintenance of correct soil pH is important when growing plants under fluorescent light.

The theory of pH is somewhat complicated—all about hydrogen ions and hydroxyl ions, etc.—and probably is understood thoroughly only by high school chemistry students and professional scientists. However, you do not really have to understand the basic pH theory of this measurable variable in order to use it to advantage, any more than you have to understand the theory of heat transfer to use a thermometer.

Basically, pH is a scale used to measure soil acidity or alkalinity. The pH scale is from 0 to 14: 0 is very acid, 14 is very alkaline, 7 is neutral, neither acid or alkaline. Each unit indicates a 10-fold increase in acidity or alkalinity, i.e., when the pH goes from 6 to 5 the acidity is increased 10-fold; when it goes from 6 to 4, the acidity is increased 100-fold.

Electrical equipment costing hundreds of dollars is used by scientists to measure pH accurately. Amateur types of pH testers (liquids or papers) can be purchased for a few dollars. These are sufficiently accurate for gardening purposes, and it is a good idea to make this small investment. These papers are not widely available—you may have to try a laboratory supply house—but garden centers sometimes have them, and occasionally a drug store carries them. Ask for Hydrion papers or pH test papers. Instructions for use come with the papers. Micro Essential Laboratory, 4224 Avenue H, Brooklyn 10,

New York, will send you a double-roll dispenser package of ♯6080 pHydrion paper for two dollars. You must give the number 6080 when ordering. The company makes pH test papers in many wide-range and short-range types for industrial, manufacturing, pharmaceutical, and other uses and they will not know what kind to send you without the number.

Most house plants grow well in slightly acid soil or other potting media with a pH of between 6 and 7, although some plants require a definitely acid soil and some demand a definitely alkaline soil. If a test shows your potting soil is too acid for the plants, add a little ground limestone. It is impossible to say just how much, but try about 1 teaspoonful to a 3-inch pot. Test again in two weeks and add a little more limestone if the pH is still too low. Experience will tell you eventually just how much you need for your particular soil. If your test shows a pH value that is too alkaline, add a little powdered sulphur—about ¼ teaspoonful to a 3-inch pot. If, during the period of adjusting the soil pH, you go too far in the opposite direction, remember that sulphur counteracts limestone, and limestone counteracts sulphur.

The correct pH enables plants to take full advantage of soil nutrients by promoting the growth of the soil micro-organisms necessary to break down nitrate fertilizers into nitrogen, and by preventing phosphorus from going into insoluble compounds and thus becoming unavailable to plants.

Plants growing in highly organic soils can stand a slightly lower value of pH than plants in soils with less organic materials. A pH value of from 6 to 7, however, is a good one to aim for, for most house plants.

If you prepare your potting soils or mixes well in advance, check the pH when you mix and again when you use the soil. This will allow time to make an initial adjustment, and a final adjustment when potting.

POTTING AND POTS

The pot in which a plant is to grow should be just big enough, in width and depth, to accommodate the root system. That may sound like an oversimplification, but it is a fact based on wide experience of plantsmen. Quite a few house plants bloom more readily when they are pot-bound or root-bound than when they are placed in pots of larger size which allow the roots to grow and ramble unrestricted.

The width and depth of pot to be used depends entirely on the size of the plant. For most plants, there should be about ½ inch of soil between root mass and wall of the pot. Roots should be allowed to fill that half inch of soil before the plant is shifted to the next size larger pot.

If there is one horticultural rule that must not be broken, it is this: do not put a potted plant in a container that does not provide a drainage exit for excess water and fertilizer solutions.

To pot or repot a plant: cover the drainage hole or holes with pieces of broken clay pot, called "crock," and cover the crock with 1 to 2 inches of gravel, vermiculite, crushed oyster shells, or similar coarse-particled material. This layer will allow water to drain through and out, but will hold the potting medium from washing out through the drainage holes or, as sometimes happens, plugging up the drainage holes. Line the pot with potting medium, in the manner of lining a baking pan with piecrust. Set the plant in the middle of the pot, at the same height at which it has been growing, and fill in around the edges with the potting soil. Leave enough space between top of soil and top of pot to accommodate water—

from a ¼ inch on small pots to as much as 1 inch on large pots. Firm the contents of the pot by tapping the pot on the table. I am a staunch advocate of the light touch in potting. Firm the soil with the fingers and tap the pot just enough to insure that roots are in contact with the medium with no air pockets (roots will not cross air spaces) and that the plant is held firmly. A wobbly plant will not grow satisfactorily because each movement breaks off some of the tiny hair roots through which the plant absorbs water and nutrients.

Tightly compacted soil around plant roots can stop a plant's growth for several weeks because it restrains root activity. Tuberous-rooted plants develop tubers of freakish, distorted forms in tightly packed soil because during growth each portion of the tuber follows the line of least resistance.

There is no limit to the kinds of containers in which plants will grow, as long as the root system is adequately accommodated and the container has provision for drainage. Sooner or later, however, most indoor gardeners conclude that they have a choice between plastic pots and clay pots. The gardener who has a heavy hand with the water bucket had best use unpainted clay pots because they are porous and aeration is better than with glazed ceramic or plastic pots.

A much better case can be made for plastic pots in an indoor garden, and I am prejudiced in their favor. I resent every minute spent in scrubbing pots, and plastic pots come clean with much less effort than clay pots. Plastic pots do not afford harbors for pest and disease organisms, as clay pots do. Plastic pots are inexpensive, light in weight, easy to store, and they bounce when dropped. Being non-porous, they do not let a plant dry out so fast as it does in a clay pot.

All ceramic containers should be sterilized before use. This can be accomplished by soaking them in a water solution of

Clorox or other household disinfectant for a few hours or over-night. I use the lazy way that cleans and sterilizes at the same time—the dishwashing machine.

Both clay and plastic pots are made in many sizes, and in several types known as standards, tubs, bulb pans, and azalea pots. A standard pot is as wide as it is deep, i.e., a 4-inch standard is 4 inches in diameter at the top and 4 inches from top of rim to bottom of pot. Tubs, bulb pans, and azalea pots are less deep than wide. The pot sizes listed in Table XI are generally available at garden centers or by mail order.

TABLE XI.
POT SIZES

Type of pot	Inside dimensions in inches Diameter	Depth	Type of pot	Inside dimensions in inches Diameter	Dept
Standard	1¼	1¼	Tub	3	2¼
	2	2		3½	2¾
	2¼	2¼		4	3
	2½	2½			
	3	3	Bulb pan	6	3¾
	3½	3½		7	3⅞
	4	4		8	4
	5	5		9	4½
	5½	5½		10	5
	6	6			
	7	7	Azalea pot	5	4
	8	8		6	4½
	9	9		7	5¼
	10	10		8	6
	12	12		10	7½
	14	14			

FERTILIZER

The *feeding* program for plants growing in a fluorescent light garden consists of providing the air, water, and light with which the plants manufacture their food. The *fertilizing* program consists of providing the nutrients absorbed by the roots.

The fluorescent light gardener, by controlling the amount and duration of light, can make his plants ignore their natural seasons and grow and thrive as if every day were the best possible day. Fertilizers are necessary to the production of high-quality house plants, and there should be no slacking off in the fertilizing program for actively growing plants, as there must be in window sill gardening to compensate for short, dull winter days. An actively growing plant should be nurtured regardless of the fact that it may be growing contrary to its natural season.

The chemical elements which must be supplied to a healthy, growing plant are principally nitrogen (as ammonium nitrate), phosphorus, and potassium.

Nitrogen is the element that gives dark green color to foliage, promotes leaf, stem, and fruit growth, improves leaf quality, produces rapid growth, and increases the protein content of plants. A plant in need of nitrogen has light green or yellowish foliage and looks sick. Too much nitrogen produces lush but weak foliage and a paucity of bloom. Nitrogen leaches away easily when plants are watered.

Phosphorus stimulates early root formation and growth, gives a rapid and vigorous start to young plants, hastens maturity, and stimulates blooming. A phosphorus deficiency may be indicated by poor root growth and delayed maturity of the above-ground portion of a plant.

Potassium (commonly referred to as potash) regulates quality by imparting increased vigor and resistance to certain diseases to plants; improves seed quality; and is essential to the formation and transfer of starches, sugars, and oils in the plant system. Potassium is markedly effective in maintaining the proper balance between nitrogen and phosphorus, retarding the too rapid growth that may take place if those two elements are too highly concentrated. Weak stems and sparse flowering may indicate a potassium deficiency in the growing medium.

Also required but in lesser quantity are sulphur, magnesium, iron, and calcium. Calcium influences absorption of plant nutrients, neutralizes acid conditions in soil, and neutralizes toxic compounds produced in plants.

All these elements enter the plant through roots in the form of solutions dissolved in water. The elements may already be present in the soil, or they can be added to the growing medium by the application of dry or liquid fertilizer compounds.

Plants need other chemical elements, the micronutrients or "trace" elements (because only a trace is needed). These are boron, molybdenum, zinc, manganese, copper, and probably others. Usually the trace elements are present in ordinary soil or as impurities in the materials used in compounding fertilizer. The indoor gardener need not be concerned about supplying trace elements if soil is used in the potting medium, or if a water-soluble house-plant fertilizer is used.

Plants differ in their nutritional requirements. A planting medium of soil, or one that contains soil, may supply sufficient nutrition for some plants but not for others. A soilless synthetic potting medium contains no nutrients. The nutritive elements applied to pot plants in the form of fertilizer may be flushed away or greatly diluted when the plants are watered, or they may accumulate in the form of salts at the surface of the potting medium when plants are watered from the bottom. All of these variable conditions require careful attention to a fertilizing schedule.

Fertilizer formulas are indicated by three numbers on the bag or bottle. The numbers indicate, in order, nitrogen, phosphorus, potassium, and the percentage of each in the mixture. The three figures total much less than 100 per cent—the difference between the total of the three elements and 100 per cent consists of inert or inactive filler materials which carry the three nutritive elements. The kind of fertilizer to use depends on the plants, and on the nutritive content of the potting medium. If a soil test shows your soil to be rich in nitrogen but low in phosphorus and potassium, you should use a fertilizer with a formula such as 0-20-10. If your soil is naturally high in potassium, a formula of 10-20-0 would probably be in order. You can test your own soil with an inexpensive soil test kit, available at garden centers or by mail order. A soil analysis can be obtained from your State Agricultural Experiment Station.

Generally, the plants suited to fluorescent light culture should be fertilized, when they are in active growth, every ten days to two weeks with a water-soluble fertilizer mixed at one-half to two-thirds the strength specified on the label. There is a good reason to err on the side of too-weak a solution: when the nutrient salts are dissolved in water, high concentrations may cause some *cells* of the plant to *lose* water, die, and become discolored as if they had been "burned."

More and more indoor gardeners who grow their plants with the aid of fluorescent light are converting their fertilizing schedule from the two or three times a month schedule to one in which they apply fertilizer every time plants are watered. The strength of fertilizer applied with such frequency must be greatly reduced—the ratio recommended is a solution that is diluted to about one-twentieth of the recommendation on the label. One successful grower has told me he uses a 30-30-30 fertilizer formula at the rate of one-sixth teaspoonful of fertilizer to a gallon of water for all watering; another alternates 10-52-17 and 34-52-17 at the rate of one-eighth teaspoonful of fertilizer to a gallon of water. A frequent, dilute solution of fertilizer is logical: consistent light of uniform duration day in and day out, and consistent fertilizing . . . one balances the other.

Fertilizing of house plants is done most conveniently with water-soluble commercial fertilizers specially prepared for house plant use. Some popular house-plant fertilizers and their formulas are listed in Tables XII-XIV.

TABLE XII.

SOLUBLE FERTILIZERS (GUARANTEED ANALYSIS)

Asgrow Soluble Fertilizer	20–20–20
Atlas Fish Emulsion	5– 1– 1
Bio-Gro Liquid Fish Fertilizer	10– 5– 5
Black Magic Liquid Fertilizer	10–15– 5
Black Magic Blossom Booster Liquid	4–10–10
Blue Whale Soluble Plant Food	6– 2– 1
Corenco Liquid Fertilizer Concentrate	5–10–10
Du Pont Soluble Plant Food	19–22–16
Gro-Stuf	20–20–20
Hyponex Plant Food	7– 6–19
Hy-Trous	4– 8– 4
Instant Vigoro	19–28–14
also	20–10–15
Miracle-Gro	15–30–15
Ortho-Gro Liquid Plant Food	10– 5– 5
Plant Marvel	12–31–14
Ra-Pid-Gro	28–21–17
Spoonit Flower Food	18–20–16
Take-Hold Starter Solution	10–52–17

TABLE XIII.

SOIL-INCORPORATED FERTILIZERS (GUARANTEED ANALYSIS)

Agrico Rose Food	5– 9–6
Agrinite	8–25–0
Armour's Sheep Manure	1¼–1–2
Asgrow Plant Food	5–10–5
Black Magic Tablets	2– 3–2
Bone meal (typical)	2–22–0
Bovung	2– 1–1
Driconure	3– 2–1
Milorganite	5½–4½–0

TABLE XIV.

SINGLE CHEMICAL FERTILIZERS (FOR DO-IT-YOURSELF
MIXING OR FORTIFYING)

Ammonium sulfate	20.6– 0– 0
Urea	46– 0– 0
Muriate of potash	0– 0–20
Nitrate of soda	16– 0– 0
Sulfate of ammonia	20– 0– 0
Potassium nitrate	14– 0–46
Triple super phosphate	0–47– 0
Urea-formaldehyde	38– 0– 0

Also available are numerous water-soluble fertilizers compounded for specific plants like cacti, gesneriads, geraniums, roses, etc. Usually, these are sold by the nurserymen who specialize in growing and selling the particular kind of plant.

It is best to apply concentrated fertilizer to a potted plant either immediately after the plant has been watered, or sometime within twelve hours of watering. You run the risk of "burning" roots and other plant parts when you apply a fertilizer solution to a plant that is in need of water.

Water-soluble fertilizer is applied to a plant the same way

as water, by pouring it on the surface of the potting medium
and letting it drain through.

Water-soluble fertilizer compounds may be mixed and stored
without loss of value or chemical change. The fertilizer elements are highly stable salts that do not change or deteriorate
in solution. It is good practice to cover the containers to prevent contamination and evaporation. A light-resistant container, as blown glass or opaque or translucent plastic, is
recommended for storing pre-mixed fertilizer solutions, but
probably is not essential.

Some house-plant fertilizers are advertised as containing
vitamins. It is not clear to me whether the manufacturers
mean to say that the fertilizers are as good for plants as vitamins
are said to be for humans, or whether they mean that the
compounds actually contain certain vitamins. Whatever the
interpretation, vitamins deteriorate in solution, and plants have
no use for vitamins anyway.

Too much fertilizer, and fertilizing at the wrong time, can
cause damage: bud blast or failure of buds to open on some
plants, browning of leaf edges on others, yellowing and dropping of leaves on still others. An insufficiency of nutrient chemicals can produce an ailing plant, too, but if a plant that has
been fertilized regularly appears to be ailing, more fertilizer
will not return it to good health.

Horticultural superstitions abound on the subject of plant
feeding and fertilizing . . . I think I have heard enough tales
of charms and magic to fill another book. Horticulture is applied botany. Botany is one of the life sciences, and there is
no place for moon signs or expended tea leaves. We need not
be botanists or any other kind of scientist to raise beautiful
plants. In fact, it seems to work the other way round: the
botanists of my acquaintance are indifferent horticulturists.
The indoor gardener needs only to provide the conditions that

a plant's nature demands. I believe that if the gardeners who swear that their great success comes from watering their plants with a liquid in which their old egg shells have been soaked, or any other such sorcery, would look again, they would find that they are observing sound horticultural principles instinctively. Probably, they are such good gardeners that the egg-shell witchcraft does no harm. More likely, they neglected to put chicken grits, oyster shells, or ground limestone in their potting soil and the egg shells supplied the calcium for which their plants were yearning.

WATER

Most ornamental plants that grow and flower so splendidly under irradiation from fluorescent lamps are extravagant in their use of water. The roots absorb it from the soil, the stem and branches circulate it through the plant, and most of it is lost into the atmosphere through pores in the leaves. This loss of moisture from plant cells by evaporation is called transpiration. The inside of a plant is a very busy place. I am rather glad that plants are not transparent. If I had to observe the continuous and swift movement of water through my plants every day, I might become too exhausted to fetch more water for them!

Of course, a plant *utilizes* some of the water taken up by its roots. As the water travels through the plant, various parts demand a portion. Water is essential to the life of plant cells; it creates the pressure inside the cells that makes the plant turgid and firm; it enlarges new cells; it encourages new root tips; it unfurls new leaves. Minerals and foods can travel and unite in the plant's complicated chemistry only when they are dissolved in water. Hydrogen and oxygen in the water combine with other elements to make sugar and hemicellulose, the building blocks of plant structures.

Even with all this utilization of water in the plant's interior, most of the water absorbed by roots is transpired into air. Leaves also exude water in drops at their tips, in a process called guttation, but this loss of water is not so serious as that of transpiration. If the supply of water is less than is needed to replace that lost through transpiration, each cell of the plant has to give up some of its share, and the plant becomes limp, wilts, and may die. So we must make sure that water is available to enter the plant roots a little more rapidly than it is lost from the leaves.

There is an underside to this matter of plant watering, too. There must be air in the soil, and if the tiny pore spaces in the soil are always filled with water, there is no room for air. Roots use the oxygen in the soil in a process called respiration, which is the act of combustion inside the cells that provides the plant with the energy to live and fulfill its function. Plants in a flooded or waterlogged pot may suffocate or drown for lack of oxygen.

Plants grow best when water and air-borne oxygen are uniformly present in soil, and they do not grow well in alternating periods of extreme dryness and extreme wetness. The most reliable way to determine whether a plant needs water is to touch the surface of the growing medium with your fingers. If it feels dry, the plant requires water. The surface, being exposed to the air, dries out ahead of the soil around the roots, but the fact that the surface has begun to dry is a signal that the plant will soon need water.

There are other ways to determine a plant's need for water. A dry plant weighs less than a moist plant, and the indoor gardener who has time to heft every pot and who can remember what it weighed the last time he lifted it may find this method satisfactory. Some planting media change color, appearing lighter when dry, and this change in appearance can be taken to indicate that water is needed. Use of a soil moisture meter is another way to ascertain the amount of moisture in the planting medium. However, such a device may mislead, because it responds not only to the moisture in the soil but also to the chemicals present in that moisture. One can get a reading of "dry" on these devices when they are placed in distilled water, which is undeniably wet. The indicator can be made to swing over the entire dial by adding pinches of salt to the distilled water.

There are two ways to water plants growing under fluorescent lights, or indeed, any plants growing any place: from the top or from the bottom.

Bottom watering employs the physical phenomenon called capillary action, in which surface tension pulls the water up under it. Do not add a wetting agent to water used for bottom watering. A wetting agent works to *decrease* surface tension, and its use would reduce or perhaps eliminate capillary action.

One form of bottom watering is to plunge a pot to its rim in a container of water, letting it stand in the water until moisture is visible on the top surface, or the surface feels damp to the touch. The pot should be removed from the water as soon as moisture reaches the top surface. Plunging is a satisfactory way to water plants in an 8-inch or larger pot, but it is also a method almost guaranteed to hurt a plant that stands in water beyond the time required to moisten the surface of the soil.

Another form of bottom watering is to put the pot in a shallow container of water, such as a saucer or tray. This method is suited to plants whose foliage hugs the pot, making

it difficult to find a place to apply water from the top, and
to those that grow with crowns that sometimes trap water
applied from above, causing the center of the plant to rot.

Wick watering is another variation of watering a plant from
the bottom. The wick is a length of fiber glass or spun glass,
long enough to reach from the inside bottom of the pot to
water in a saucer, tray, or other container.

A disadvantage of bottom watering is the ever-present danger
of forgetting that one has left a plant sitting in water, and
discovering a day or two later that it is in a boggy condition,
limp and drowning from lack of air-borne oxygen. A more
serious disadvantage, because one does not notice it, is the
accumulation of salts on the surface of the soil. These deposits
are carried to the surface by the rising water. When bottom
watering is the method preferred, it should be alternated about
once a month with a thorough watering from the top.

Top watering is the natural way by which most plants are
watered in the wild. It employs both capillary attraction and
the force of gravity to pull the water down through the soil
to the bottom of the pot. As it travels downward, water is
absorbed by the potting medium which in turn makes the
water with its cargo of dissolved nutrients available to plant
roots. Water not absorbed and not needed flows away through
the holes in the bottom of the pot. Room is normally left for
the air-borne oxygen required by a plant's roots.

Nature perfected this system of supplying water to plants
by applying it from the top a long time ago. I think it is the
best way to water potted plants. Foliage does not water spot
or burn under fluorescent light if water is used at room temperature, as it sometimes does when sunlight strikes wet leaves,
so precautions to avoid wetting the foliage are not so vital.

Top watering is accomplished by applying water to the
surface of the potting medium until the water runs through

the drainage holes in the bottom of the pot. Not an eyedropper-ful every morning to let the plants know you are thinking of them, not a deluge once a month after a plant has wilted, but a thorough watering from the top that will drain through and out the bottom, applied when the surface of the soil looks or feels dry.

It should be noted that chemical salts accumulate on the surface when top watering is employed, as they do with bottom watering. They are brought to the surface by the evaporation of water from the potting medium. However, as regularly as they accumulate they are flushed away by the next top watering and do not pile up to the point of harming the plant, except when hard water is used that eventually crusts the pot rims with insoluble calcium salts.

The frequency of watering depends on the "weather" in the plant room and on each plant's water requirements. Not all plants in an indoor garden need water at the same time. When I observe that a particular plant dries out quickly day after day, I take it as a signal that this plant needs a larger pot, or the potting medium needs more of some moisture-retentive ingredient such as sphagnum peat or vermiculite.

Plants in a fluorescent light garden should be watered when the temperature is rising, which is the time of their greatest need for water. When I have the time to water my plants in the morning, after the lights are turned on, I usually also mist the foliage with the same tepid water. More often than not, however, my plants are watered in the evening, because that is when I am at home and have time to tend plants. When watering is done shortly before the lights are to be turned off, I try not to get water on foliage or flowers. Wet foliage in darkness provides an excellent breeding ground for disease organisms.

Use tepid water for indoor plants. The water need not be at

a precise stipulated temperature, so long as it is within ten degrees above or below the temperature of the room. One gardener of my acquaintance keeps gallon bottles filled with water in several spots throughout his indoor garden, so there is always room temperature water available. A battery filler or a large baster is in the neck of each bottle, making a quick and satisfactory way to water any plant when it needs it.

Tepid water can usually be used as it comes from the tap. Highly chlorinated water, however, should be allowed to stand in the open overnight before use, to permit the water to become degassified. Chlorine does not damage plants directly, but it does destroy the micro-organisms that work on fertilizer elements to make the elements available to plants.

Note, please, that if you have a water softener of the ion-exchange type, such as Zeolite, the water for plants should be removed from the water line *before* it goes into the softener. This kind of softener replaces the calcium in water with sodium. Sodium is toxic to plants, accumulates in the soil, does not settle out, evaporate, or become harmless, and cannot be removed from the soil.

When watering a potted plant that grows from a bulb, tuber, or corm, it is usually better to apply the water around the edge and not directly into the center of the pot. Most bulbs, tubers, and corms have depressions in which water is easily trapped, leading to rotting.

PLANT ENEMIES

Sanitation is as important a factor as light, temperature, or humidity in a fluorescent light garden. It is easier to prevent trouble than it is to cure it.

Use pasteurized potting mixes, sterilize all containers and tools; space plants so leaves do not touch; use care in watering and fertilizing; do not let foliage stay wet for more than a few hours; wash plants thoroughly under a spray of tepid water every couple of weeks; use an insecticide/fungicide spray at least once a month.

Isolate new plants until you are sure they bear no pests or diseases. Immediately remove and isolate from the other plants any plant that shows signs of distress. When you bring a plant home from an exhibit or show, do not put it near your other plants right away—it may have won a blue ribbon in the show but it may also have picked up some contamination from the losers.

Wash your hands after you have handled an infested or diseased plant—many of the pests and diseases of house plants are transferred from plant to plant by the gardener. You might touch an infested plant in a friend's collection without knowing it and carry minute pests home to a beautiful collection.

Groom your plants regularly, removing and discarding spent flowers and dying foliage. Decaying plant material is a culture medium for botrytis mold and other disease organisms. Put it in the garbage or the incinerator.

An indoor fluorescent light garden does not have to be run on the same high standards of hygiene as a surgical room in a hospital, of course, but a bottle of Clorox or another household disinfectant kept handy in the plant room or garden area and used full strength to wipe the working surfaces and pots is a precaution you will not regret.

Above all, be vigilant in plant inspection. Pick up the pots and look at the plants from all sides, especially the undersides of leaves. Do it often. Do not assume that because you have never seen a pest in your indoor garden, you never will. The gardener who says, "Bugs? Not on my plants!" usually is bitten the hardest, and you will please excuse the bad pun.

For sheer mass terror, I have never seen anything to match the panic on the faces of twenty-five or so people at a plant society meeting, when one of their number came into the room holding up an African violet that was infested with cyclamen mite. The man inquired mildly if anyone might know what was the matter with his plant, because he had lots more at home just like it and thought he ought to do *something*. A bagful of mice turned loose under the chairs would not have scattered those ladies as quickly as the sick plant did. The poor fellow was told what he could do with his plant—burn it, bury it, destroy it, but get it away from the other plants fast—and he was shunned like the plague for the rest of the evening.

Insects are classified according to their mouth parts—chewing or sucking types—and they may be controlled by a knowledge of their feeding habits. Chewing insects eat holes in leaves, chew or cut off stems, or burrow into stems and eat their way along until the stem breaks off or dies. Sucking insects suck the juices from the leaves or stem, causing leaves to curl and turn brown or the plant to wilt or die.

Plant diseases consist primarily of fungi and bacteria. Fungous and bacterial diseases of foliage are not commonly found on house plants. When they do develop, it is usually after long periods of wet foliage. Most house-plant diseases affect roots and lower stems, and develop most often in heavy, poorly drained soils.

A combination spray that contains insecticides for the insects and fungicides for the diseases is convenient to use and is recommended. Many successful indoor gardeners make it a practice to spray their plants with one of these all-purpose plant sprays once a month, whether the plants need it or not. I do so once a week.

The windows and doors in a plant room or indoor garden area should be screened. Fluorescent lights attract some summer insects. The insects are more annoying than dangerous, but they can thoroughly upset a hybridizing program. If you use a ventilating system that pulls air from the outside through the plant room, do not plant just outside the windows anything that is host to the kinds of insects that also like house plants. For example, thrips and gladioli go together, so do thrips and gloxinias, and thrips can be pulled through the finest mesh screen.

It is impractical to list here the pests and diseases that may attack all the different kinds of plants grown in fluorescent light gardens. Books dealing with general house-plant culture or with a plant family, genus, or species, usually include full descriptions of and control recommendations for the pests and diseases that may bother a particular kind of plant. Several such books are listed in the bibliography of this book.

I have planted, Apollos watered; but God gave the increase.
I Corinthians, I, 27

7

Plant Propagation

If by some stroke of circumstance or limitation of space, I were to be severely restricted in my use of fluorescent light for indoor gardening, I would employ what lamps I had for propagating plants. It is the joy of the fluorescent light gardener to be able to grow the rarest of tropical plants from seeds and cuttings.

The bottom bench in each of the 3-decked tiers of benches in our plant factory is equipped as a propagating bench. The shelf is completely enclosed in plastic sheeting stapled to the uprights at the corners and along the bottom of the bench above. The plastic at the front of the bench is stapled only to the bottom of the bench above so it can be lifted or rolled up out of the way, or dropped like a curtain. A hem was stapled across the bottom of the plastic and a broom handle slipped through the hem. The pole weights the plastic so it does not flutter when you walk by, and provides something on which to roll the plastic curtain up and out of the way when I want to work at the bench.

The bench is lined first with plastic film, then with tarpaper for insulation. The insulation is a felty, asphalt-impregnated paper sometimes called builder's paper, available from a lumber yard for less than three dollars for a 3 by 100-foot roll. A 60-foot General Electric heating cable is laid in position on top of the builder's paper and covered with an inch of sand. Do not use peat or vermiculite directly on top of a heating cable—both substances have insulating qualities that restrict the distribution of heat to the propagating medium. Over the sand is a 3- to 4-inch layer of a propagating mixture. My particular benches each take about 4 cubic feet of material. I use Albert Buell's propagating mix, and also Black Magic planter mix to which an equal amount of horticultural vermiculite is added.

The heating cable is controlled by a thermostat probe which is buried in the mixture at about the center of the bench, and the control dial for the thermostat is fastened to the outside of the bench in an accessible spot. The thermostat for the heating cable is usually set at about 75 degrees F., and the air temperature in the enclosure is usually between 85 and 90 degrees F.

The fluorescent lights for the propagating bench are on the same time-control switch as the other benches. Some indoor gardeners and some published authorities recommend that the lights over a propagating unit be burned continuously around the clock, and I understand that this works satisfactorily. I try, however, to follow the practices of Nature in all of my horticultural activities, and since Nature usually allows night to fall on plants, I do likewise and give the propagating areas 16 hours of light and 8 hours of darkness.

I like to use Gro-Lux lamps exclusively for all plant propagation. The lights are any distance from 6 to 11 inches above the tops of cuttings or surface of the seed bed. My experience with Gro-Lux lamps for plant propagation—and I have repeated the experience many, many times—is that cuttings root faster and seedlings develop substantial, healthy root systems more quickly than under any of the white fluorescent lamps. The plants get off to a fine, healthy start.

This large enclosed propagating area is a vital adjunct to my other fluorescent light gardening. Not only is it used for the rooting of cuttings and starting of seeds, but also for starting potted tubers and bulbs into growth, and as the home of mature potted plants that require warm, moist growing conditions, such as some orchids and *Begonia luxurians*.

When the space is not needed for plant propagation, I turn off the heating cable, roll up the plastic curtain, place wire lath platforms over the propagating mixture, and use the bench for growing potted plants.

SEEDS

Seed germination processes are dependent upon the factors of temperature, moisture, oxygen, and light. The temperature for seed germination should be about 10 degrees higher than is required for normal growth of the plant. The presence of water softens the seed coat, permitting water accompanied by oxygen to enter the seed. Enzyme reaction and the necessary life processes are hastened, respiration increases, stored food in the seed is translocated—all resulting in growth of the embryo and the initial formation of the primary root. Light requirements are definite for many seeds.

For propagating plants from seeds, I use a variety of small electric propagating cases. My favorite method is to sow the seeds on top of moist *milled* sphagnum moss, in individual plastic ice-cube cups, mist lightly to anchor the seeds to the moss, and place the ice-cube cups in an electric propagating case. Some of my propagating cases have their own fluorescent light hoods. The cases with a transparent plastic cover are placed on one of the growing benches under the lights.

I do not wait for the customary four leaves to appear on seedlings before transplanting them, but move the tiny plants from the seed bed to a small flat as soon as I can get hold of them. The seed containers are removed from the bottom heat about three days after germination is visible, but kept enclosed in plastic, under lights, for two to three days more. Then the seedlings are transplanted to small flats, still enclosed in plastic, and placed about 6 inches under the lamps. I make no attempt to separate the tiny roots from the moss, but transplant whatever amount of moss adheres to the roots. Sometimes I remove a few seedlings at a time from the milled sphagnum moss, getting successive bloom from one batch of seed. The seedlings will "hold" in the sphagnum moss more or less indefinitely, or they will grow there if fertilized. Sometimes a white mold appears on the surface of the sphagnum moss, as a result of the heat and moisture, but the mold is harmless and can be ignored.

I use a great many of the miniature plastic greenhouses (Union Products, Inc.) to house the little ice-cube cups that contain batches of seed. I wish I could limit myself on the number of batches of seed, but who can resist trying something new? I always seem to have sixty-leven batches under way, and the miniature greenhouses provide the necessary enclosure to retain humidity. They are transparent so the light gets to the seeds and seedlings, and they can be placed directly on any source of bottom heat. The small plastic flats to which I transplant seedlings from the seed beds are the bases of the miniature plastic greenhouses, drilled with drainage holes. The larger size holds fifteen seedlings spaced about 1 inch apart. The plants grow in the miniature greenhouses until the leaves touch, at which time plants are potted up individually.

A fluorescent light garden offers another made-to-order spot for seed germination. Feel along the top of a fluorescent light fixture for the warm area near the ballast of the fixture, and place there small containers of seeds enclosed in plastic. The light in such areas, of course, is reflected and not direct light, but it is adequate for starting most of the seeds of plants to be used for bedding plants out of doors. The bottom heat is ideal.

CUTTINGS

A cutting is any part that has been cut from a plant and is capable of regeneration. This method of propagation is vital for cultivars, the plants that do not come true from seed.

The stem of a leaf cutting should be at least ½ inch long to anchor the leaf in the rooting medium. Medium mature leaves—not the youngest and not the oldest—produce the best plants.

One-third to one-half the length of a tip cutting should be inserted in the rooting medium, which should be firmed around the base of the cutting. There should be sufficient space between cuttings in the rows and between rows of cuttings for circulation of air. The temperature of the rooting medium should be 70 to 75 degrees, the air temperature about 10 degrees higher. The relative humidity in the air surrounding the cuttings should be at least 60 per cent. The rooting medium should be kept moist. Moisture keeps the cuttings turgid, and maintains absorption, translocation, and photosynthetic activity. Light plays an important part in photosynthesis.

Some cuttings can be rooted only in water, and some root more quickly in water than in a rooting medium. Often I have found that cuttings taken from a plant that has been grown

on the dry side must be rooted in water. For water-rooting purposes, I use the little glass and plastic bottles that headache
tablets and prescription pills are packaged in. I push the water-
filled vial down into the bottom-heated rooting medium and put
the cutting in the vial.

The use of hormone powders to assist cuttings to root surely
and quickly is a matter to be decided by each indoor gardener
for himself. I rarely use the powders, but many gardeners consider them essential.

Cuttings should be potted up when they have developed
½- to ¾-inch roots. If permitted to grow in the rooting medium
or water to a larger size, the new plants suffer a setback when
finally transferred to a pot.

Time

The time required for seeds to germinate and cuttings to
root varies considerably with different kinds of plants, with the
viability of seeds, and with the condition of cuttings. I waited
thirteen months for one solitary tea-plant seed to germinate.
I came to loathe the sound of the word, tea, after looking at
the little ice-cube cup in which the seed was planted every day
for so many months.

I have learned, through the process of losing rare seeds, to
read before planting. Books on house-plant culture and on the
culture of various individual kinds of plants describe the propagating conditions and requirements for the plants.

And not by eastern windows only,
When daylight comes, comes in the light.
ARTHUR HUGH CLOUGH

8

Other Applications of Fluorescent Light to Garden Areas

In addition to their use for growing plants in an apartment, dwelling, garage, or basement, fluorescent lights are used to supplement or replace daylight in other situations.

IN THE HOME GREENHOUSE

In my own hobby greenhouse, I use fluorescent lamps to supplement natural light on cloudy or dull days throughout the year.

Fluorescent light fixtures with reflectors (2-tube, 40-watt industrials) are suspended by chains from the greenhouse roof over the benches. Attached to each fixture is a light-sensitive switch (photo-electric switch) that turns the lights on automatically when the level of natural light drops, and switches them off when it brightens again. On a day of in-and-out sunshine, the lights in the greenhouse go on when the sun is obscured by a cloud and off again when the cloud passes. Thus the lights may turn on and off many times in one day, or stay on all day in rainy, dull weather. On bright days the lights may not turn on at all.

The greenhouse is attached to the house, with a picture window between. The bench on the greenhouse side of the window is dressed with the prettiest plants and flowers in the greenhouse. I long to get home from work at dusk on midwinter evenings and walk into the darkened living room, because I know the light-sensitive switch will have turned the lights on in the adjoining greenhouse. The Gro-Lux lamps over the tulips, hyacinths, iris, camellias, and other cool-growing plants make a picture window display that is prettier than an artist's painting, rivaling anything I have ever seen in a florist's showcase. This living picture window is, in truth, the most beautiful, soul-satisfying picture I have ever seen. I have it every day and I can rearrange it at my and the plants' will.

We do not have a time-control switch on our greenhouse fixtures, so we must remember to turn on power manually to the fluorescent lights early in the morning and turn it off in the late evening. The result, of course, is a longer day in the greenhouse than we would get from natural winter light. I will like it better when we connect the greenhouse fluorescent light fixtures to a time control switch.

The light-sensitive switch mentioned is an industrial type, purchased from an electrical supply dealer for about ten dollars, and it should be installed in a fluorescent light power-supply circuit by an electrician. However, just as satisfactory is a domestic light-sensitive switch, the kind used to turn house lights on at dusk and off at dawn to scare away burglars. Plug the fixture into the switch and the switch into the electrical outlet. Some trade names for domestic switches are "Nite Liter"

FIG. 32 Picture window between living room and greenhouse of author's home. Fluorescent fixture in greenhouse is controlled by a photo electric switch which turns the lamps on whenever the sunlight falls below a pre-set level. A dramatic picture at night.

[*Photo by Bernice Brilmayer*]

and "Electric Eye," and they cost about ten dollars at department stores, or from Mongomery Ward or Sears Roebuck.

All electrical equipment used in a greenhouse, whether portable or installed permanently, should be electrically grounded. If the greenhouse frame is metal, it too should be grounded. I repeat: *never use any piece of ungrounded electrical equipment in a greenhouse.* Disregard of this safety precaution could result in electrocution if you happened to be standing in water and touching an electrical apparatus at an instant when the wiring failed. You have undoubtedly heard of accidents like this happening to people using electric drills. I am not trying to frighten you away from an electrified greenhouse, only to make sure you will be around a long, long time to enjoy it.

In a greenhouse, the glass roof allows natural light to enter the interior in the daytime, but at night artificial light will escape through the glass. Because of this, fluorescent light fixtures in a greenhouse should have reflectors.

The dark areas under benches in a greenhouse can be converted to fluorescent light gardens by installing shelves and hanging fixtures from the bottom of the benches. Some commercial growers do this successfully, almost doubling the available growing space in their greenhouses. It is not practical in my hobby greenhouse because the misting nozzles that maintain the relative humidity in the greenhouse are located on the ground under the benches. I would rather have this humidifying system than more fluorescent light gardens, at least in this particular location.

TO SUPPLEMENT NATURAL LIGHT IN A WINDOW GARDEN

Suspend a fluorescent light fixture over plants growing on a window sill. Turn the light on during the day whenever natural light reaching the plants through the windows is at a

FIG. 33 Second-hand commercial fluorescent light fixtures were painted and suspended in pipe rack frames. Photo taken at exhibit of author's plants, North Shore Horticultural Society.

low level, as in cloudy or rainy weather. Also use the fluorescent light after natural darkness falls, to extend the day length of the plants.

TO DISPLAY PLANTS

Plants may be displayed for a few days or even weeks in areas in which they might not grow well. The 15- and 20-watt fluorescent lamps that are inadequate for the growing of plants are quite suitable for plant display. Attractive fluorescent light units are available: self-supporting fixtures, fixtures that can be suspended over a table, and combination fixture and tray or planter units.

The fluorescent lamp called "natural white" (Sylvania) emits a high level of red light that greatly enhances the beauty of plants. Yet the general impression of this lamp is one of soft light, pleasant and comfortable to look at.

Gro-Lux lamps are ideal for displaying plants, but the funereal lavender glow might irritate a person trying to relax.

The light from a fluorescent desk lamp will sustain a specimen plant in flowering condition for several weeks.

TO IMPROVE SHOW PLANTS

Often the appearance and condition of a window-sill or greenhouse plant being grown and groomed for exhibit or competition can be improved considerably by a few days' fluorescent light irradiation. When a plant looks as if the buds will not quite be open by the exhibit date, put the plant under fluorescent light for a few days prior to the show. It does not always work, but it does often enough to be worth trying.

Not too many years ago, it was felt that the indoor gardener with fluorescent lights had an unfair advantage over the window-sill gardener, and artificially irradiated plants sometimes were not allowed to compete with plants grown in natural light. So far as I have been able to determine, however, most horticultural shows and exhibits no longer discriminate against plants grown under fluorescent light. Fluorescent light culture is now an accepted way to grow indoor plants.

FIG. 34 An African violet is maintained in flowering condition for several weeks by the light from a fluorescent desk lamp, home of Mr. and Mrs. Paul Arnold.

TERRARIUMS

A terrarium is an enclosure of glass or plastic for keeping or raising plants or animals indoors. My terrariums—small, medium, large—are the sparkling jewels in my fluorescent light creatures in my terrariums. Three Irish setters, uncounted tropical fish, a yard full of birds and squirrels, and the neighbors' cats are quite enough mouths for one household to feed.

But there are many kinds of plants in different stages of growth living happily in the protective atmosphere of our various terrariums.

Sometimes I improvise a terrarium on the spur of the moment by inverting a drinking glass over a small plant that seems to be signaling that it would like "a more humid home, please," or by swathing an individual plant in plastic. The miniature plastic greenhouses mentioned earlier are, in effect, terrariums. From some unremembered source I acquired several small glass coffee servers that make fine terrariums for individual plants. I have several pieces of glassware and transparent plastic ware shaped like brandy snifters, and a glass jar which the donor thinks I am using for cocktail crackers, and small round fish bowls. Any of these containers that do not have their own transparent plastic or glass covers are fitted with a piece of glass or more often with a piece of clinging transparent food-wrap material, such as Saran Wrap. Also, I use rectangular fish tanks from the 2½-gallon size to the 20-gallon size as terrariums.

All terrariums are placed on the benches under fluorescent lights, among the potted plants, except the largest fish tanks that have their own 2-tube 20-watt fixtures and lights.

The attention-getter among my terrariums is a street-light globe 18 inches in diameter, acquired for three dollars from a local florist who had been using it to cover dried-flower arrangements. I use it with the opening at the top, and balance the round bottom on a coil of aluminum lawn-edging material. My husband built a square tray-type hood of ¼-inch plywood in which he installed a 22-watt circline fluorescent light fixture and lamp. The hood is inverted over the globe terrarium, and the circline lamp rests on the glass rim. I guess I was just lucky that the opening in the globe has the same diameter as the circline lamp.

Terrariums should be kept sparkling clean to make them look beautiful and to allow maximum light for the enclosed plants. Ventilation should be provided by lifting or removing the cover for a few hours to permit escape of the excess moisture that accumulates on the inside walls of the containers.

AQUARIUMS

We have used fluorescent lighting over our indoor aquariums for as long as we have had the aquariums, and now we use Gro-Lux lamps.

An interior wall between the living room and my study was deliberately constructed with openings for various sizes of fish tanks. On the living-room side, the tanks are flush with the wall. On the study side, the wall is lined with shelves that support the tanks, the fluorescent light fixtures, and the aerating equipment. The tanks are serviced from the study side of the wall. Some sections of the shelves hold books, and several sections are set up with small fluorescent light gardens. Much too often, I find myself admiring the plants and staring back at the fish when I should be whipping the typewriter to meet an editor's deadline.

I will not attempt instructions on the operation and maintenance of indoor aquariums—that would be another book—except to say that a tank should be lighted from the top, not from the sides. In nature, water creatures receive their light from above, and you may find yourself with some very confused fish if you put lights at the sides of a tank. Fish are simple creatures to begin with, and they cannot handle a situation that requires intelligence or much adaptation.

The oxygenating and ornamental plants usually found in hobby aquariums grow beautifully in a tank illuminated with

FIG. 35 Miniature tropical water lily 'Margaret Mary'.

[*Three Springs Fisheries*]

fluorescent light. We have not bought new plants for our tanks in over three years—we just prune off the growth that constantly appears on the old plants. Plants recommended are *Cabomba, Myriophyllum* (water-milfoil), *Anacharis, Ludwigia,* and *Ceratophyllum demersum* (hornwort).

Particularly recommended for an indoor aquarium is a new miniature water lily, 'Margaret Mary', from Three Springs Fisheries, Lilypons, Maryland. 'Margaret Mary' is a viviparous plant (young plants develop from the centers of mature leaves). Star-shaped light blue flowers with deep golden centers are about the size of a half-dollar. The floating lily pads are about 3 inches in diameter. The lily is dependable enough in blooming habits to be suitable for year-around indoor culture, and gets along very well in a 10- or 20-gallon tank with a minimum of four hours daily exposure to Gro-Lux light suspended 3 to 4 inches above the lily pads.

The visual effect of Gro-Lux lamps on tropical fish must be seen to be believed. You will discover in your fish brilliant colorations that are not visible in natural light or in light from white fluorescent lamps. I do not know very much about the technical details of the light requirements of fish, except that we have some ancient and honorable specimens, in terms of piscatorial life expectancy, swimming around happy as clams at high tide in our fluorescent lighted liquid jewel cases.

PART THREE

The Plants

All that in this delightfull Gardin growes,
Should happie be, and have immortall blis.

To everything there is a season, and a time
to every purpose under the heaven.

Ecclesiastes, III, 1

9

Plants for
the Fluorescent Light Garden

A dear, skeptical friend—may I know him forever—visits
my fluorescent light gardens regularly. He is a greenhouse man
to the soul, and he longs to be able to point triumphantly to
a plant and say, "I *knew* it wouldn't grow without sunlight!"
He has not been able to make that remark yet, but still he
will not give in and admit that fluorescent lights can replace
natural light completely in the growing of plants, even while
he stands grudgingly admiring a jungle of beautiful plants and
flowers. His standard disgruntled comment as he leaves the
indoor gardens is always, "You sure do beat those plants back
into their pots with all that light."

My friend's remark is valid. The house plant enthusiast who
starts to grow his plants under fluorescent lights after having
had reasonable success growing them on a window sill or in
a greenhouse will notice an outstanding difference soon after
starting fluorescent light culture: plants mature, bud and flower
while they are younger, smaller and more compact than they

do when they are grown in available natural light. There is a reason for this.

The stem, as well as all the leaves of a plant, is sensitive to light. When grown in sunlight, inner leaves receive less light than outer ones. Lower leaves are shaded by the upper leaves that receive more direct light. Also, the outer leaves show a preferential absorption of some colors of light, which changes the composition of the light received by the inner leaves.

Usually the leaves of a plant reach out in all directions. To achieve uniform irradiation, the lighting should be arranged to reach the leaves with the same intensity from each direction. Nature, however, does not manage this out of doors, and it is not practical to try to do it in an indoor fluorescent light garden.

The manner in which leaves absorb light explains why the rosette types of plants grow so beautifully under fluorescent lights. The leaves of African violets, gloxinias, and many other gesneriads lie in the same horizontal plane, close to the pot. It is a simple matter to irradiate them uniformly from above. Plants with leaves that grow in a vertical plane—orchids, for example—would best be irradiated from two or more sides. The nuisance of arranging fluorescent tubes at the sides of plants rules out side lighting in most indoor gardens. Instead of *direct* light from the sides, the plants receive *reflected* light— not the perfect arrangement but good enough.

Start your fluorescent light culture with the lamps about 50 per cent farther above the tops of the plants than is recommended in the list of plants that follows. Gradually lower the lamps, or raise the plants, if the foliage appears to be reaching up to the light when it should be growing outward. This treatment is better than shocking the plants with an abrupt abundance of light.

Plants placed under the ends of fluorescent lamps develop more slowly than those placed under the centers of the tubes.

Some varieties of plants grow faster and get bigger than others of the same genus or species, even of the same seed lot. A group of 50 to 100 seedlings developed from one seed pod, especially if the seeds were the result of hybrid parentage, may show such diversity of size, habit, and response to light and cultural requirements that it is hard to believe they are even related. It is the nature of some plant groups to be quite different one from another.

There can be no recipe that says you must *always* place a certain kind of plant a specified measured number of inches from the lamps. Generally, a plant receiving insufficient light develops foliage that grows up, up toward the light. The foliage of a plant receiving more light than it needs may be light- to yellow-green in color and it grows downward to hug the pot. Cultural directions for growing house plants in a greenhouse or on a window sill in natural light sometimes state that a plant is naturally shade-loving or that it will not tolerate direct sun. I have found that these so-called shade-loving plants enjoy full fluorescent light very much. I suspect that it is not the sun's *light* from which they try to escape but the sun's *heat*.

The window-sill necessity of turning a plant a quarter of the way around every day or so to provide equal light distribution to retain symmetry is eliminated with fluorescent light culture, except that plants at the extreme outer edges of a lighted growing area may need this attention occasionally.

Bud blast (the browning and dying of unopened flower buds) may be caused by insects but on a healthy plant occurs when some environmental factor is out of balance with the plant's requirements. When a plant is subjected to an unfavorable condition, the first thing it does to protect its existence is rid itself of unnecessary parts. It sloughs off the buds because it has not enough or too much of something to support the buds and itself, too. The unfavorable factor could be insufficient or too much of a vital condition such as humidity, light, or fertilizer; too high or too low a temperature; too big or too small a pot; or a draft of air falling on the plant. It could be a pest or a disease on the buds or in some other portion of the plant. Or it could be more than one of these. When buds blast, you can be sure that the plant's requirements are unsatisfied, due to something you are doing or something you are not doing. The factor most commonly at fault is insufficient humidity. The next most common fault is insufficient light (though this can usually be recognized more by absence of budding than by bud blast). The third is probably a temperature extreme, either too high or too low. My first gloxinias were grown from tubers. The humidity, temperature, and light were correct, but the pots were too small and the soil too heavy to accommodate the roots. The result was blasted flower buds.

If a mature plant does not flower in your fluorescent light garden, and you know you are meeting its cultural requirements, the trouble is likely to be that the plant needs a different length of darkness than you are giving it. A knowledge of a plant's native environment sometimes helps in determining the light and dark requirements of species plants; however, many hybrids do not inherit their parents' light requirements and often prove to be day neutral.

One of the best things about fluorescent light gardening is that parts of a plant may touch the lamps without being burned or singed, as they would be if they touched an incandescent bulb or when sunlight strikes wet foliage. I have on occasion become impatient with plants that I felt really ought to be flowering, and have boosted the plants up so the foliage touched the tubes. This procedure is highly successful with smithianthas —the strong irradiation seems to draw the buds and flowers right out of a reluctant plant. I have a plant of *Cissus striata* that cannot resist the attraction of fluorescent light. It twines its tendrils right around the tube. I pinch off new growth so the plant will not creep inside the fixture and beneath this vine-encircled lamp I place plants with low-level light requirements.

ORNAMENTAL PLANTS

In a book of this size it is impractical to give detailed descriptions and cultural information for every kind of plant I have grown or could recommend to grow in your fluorescent light garden. I hope that you already know the cultural requirements of favorite plants, or can learn to grow them from the publications of plant societies and from books on houseplant culture.

In the following list some of the most popular house plants, which are also some of the easiest and most beautiful for fluorescent light culture, are described and their culture under lights is prescribed in detail. Many other unrelated plants are described briefly, with the following terms used to prescribe culture:

Light duration. LONG DAY is 16 to 18 hours of fluorescent light in every 24 hours. DAY NEUTRAL is 14 to 16 hours of fluorescent light. SHORT DAY is 6 to 8 hours of fluorescent light.

Light intensity. Stated in inches between top of plant and any of the white fluorescent lamps (cool white, warm white, daylight, etc.).

Temperature. Given for daytime; night temperatures should drop ten degrees but not, of course, below 32 degrees Fahrenheit. COOL is 40 to 60 degrees daytime—plants with this requirement usually do best under fluorescent lights on a cool porch, in a cool greenhouse, or in an unused room in which the temperature can be kept down. MODERATE is 50 to 70 degrees daytime—usually the basement or an unused room is best for plants requiring this temperature range. WARM is 60 to 80 degrees daytime—the majority of house plants listed fall in this temperature range, which is an average condition found in most homes.

All temperature figures mentioned in this book are in degrees Fahrenheit, the temperature scale most used in the United States. The following conversion formulas will be helpful to those who garden in countries or areas using the Celsius or centigrade temperature scale: Fahrenheit $= 9/5$ centigrade $+ 32$; conversely, centigrade $= 5/9$ (Fahrenheit $- 32$).

Relative humidity. 50 to 55 per cent unless otherwise stated.

Soil Medium. ALL PURPOSE MIX may be my mix or one of the soilless mixes described in Chapter 6, or a prepared tropical plant mix. EPIPHYTIC MIX may be 3 parts peat moss, 3 parts perlite, 1 part chopped charcoal; or coarse sphagnum moss or osmunda fiber with or without chopped charcoal. DESERT MIX may be my all-purpose mix with 2 parts of sand instead of 1 part, or the mix you like best for cacti and other succulent plants.

Water. DRY—let the medium dry thoroughly before watering. MOIST—water when the soil in the top of the pot feels dry to the touch. WET—never allow the soil to dry.

Fertilizer. Every 10 days when plant is in growth, or with a very weak fertilizer solution (Chapter 6) every time the plant is watered. Only the exceptions to this fertilizing schedule are noted in the listing of plants.

Gesneriad culture. Plant does well with the culture prescribed for gesneriads, page 186.

Succulent culture. Plant is of a water-retentive nature and requires succulent culture, page 164, regardless of the family it belongs to.

Propagation. Methods of propagation are noted in order of preference.

Few plants put on a continuous, glorious twelve-month show of flowers. A plant will not produce buds and flowers before it has accumulated an excess of sugars and starches. Many plants bloom off and on during the year, others are evergreen but flower just once or twice a year, and some require definite dormant periods before they will bloom again. Usually, a plant that grows from a tuber, rhizome, bulb, or corm requires a period of dormancy after flowering. The fibrous-rooted plants usually grow the year around. Plants should be rested, pruned or cut back, or discarded, according to their individual natures.

The information that follows comes from experience—mostly my own, but some, where credited, is that of other devoted fluorescent light gardeners.

Plants are listed in alphabetical order. The botanical (Latin) name is at the left, printed in bold face italics. The word in light face italics is the name of the family to which the plant belongs. The third name, printed in roman type, is the common name of the plant when one is known. To locate a plant known to you only by its common name, consult the Index.

Abutilon   *Malvaceae*   Flowering Maple

Drooping hollyhock-like flowers the year around on woody plants. Plants tend to legginess and should be kept potbound with supplemental fertilizing to make up for the root restriction. Start new plants about every six months. Pinch growing tips of young plants to encourage fullness and a multitude of flowering tips. Recommended: *A. Savitzii, A. striatum* var. *Thompsonii.*

Day neutral, 4 inches, moderate, all purpose medium, moist. Propagate by cuttings or seeds.

Acacia   *Leguminosae*

Short-lived little trees which produce yellow flowers for about three months. Discard plants after flowering and start new plants from seeds each year. Plants grow rapidly. Recommended: *A. Baileyana, A. lophantha (Albizzia lophantha).*

Day neutral, 3 to 4 inches, cool—not above 50° daytime and can go to 25° night, all purpose medium kept moist. Propagate by seeds; cuttings are difficult to root.

Acalypha   *Euphorbiaceae*

Showy tropical shrubs that flower the year around. Prune roots and tops to keep plants manageable. Recommended: *A. hispida (A. Sanderi),* red hot cattail or chenille plant, bright red flowers in long pendant spikes; *A. Wilkesiana* var. *Macafeana,* commonly called copper leaf, insignificant flowers but the red, copper and green leaves are greatly enhanced by the fluorescent light.

Day neutral, 3 to 6 inches, warm, wilts easily in a dry atmosphere and does best with minimum 60% humidity, all purpose medium, moist at all times. Propagate by cuttings, preferably heel cuttings.

Acanthus mollis   *Acanthaceae*   Bears Breech,
Architectural Plant

Primarily a foliage plant but under lights it produces from the top of the plant a four-sided spike of whitish flowers. Give a short semi-dry rest away from the lights after flowering.

Day neutral, 9 inches, moderate, all purpose medium, moist. Propagate by seeds or division of the rhizome.

Achimenes   *Gesneriaceae*   Magic Flower

Fibrous-rooted with scaly rhizomes, trailing or much-branched upright plants, free blooming in many colors. One specialist lists more than a hundred species and hybrids. The rhizomes multiply prodigiously in one growing season. Especially recommended: *A. Andrieuxii,* a species of dwarf habit and compact stature that will produce many violet and white flowers like miniature gloxinias when grown in a 3-inch pot; *A. Ehrenbergii,* a dwarf, compact plant with bright green leaves densely woolly underneath and lavender gloxinia-like flowers for six to eight months; A. 'Purple King', magnificent purple flowers in profusion for four to six months.

Day neutral, 4 inches, warm, an all purpose medium that must never be allowed to dry out, 60% humidity. Achimenes will go into dormancy if the growing medium dries out, regardless of their stage of growth. After flowering, dry off the rhizomes, clean them, and store in vermiculite in a plastic bag for two to three months. Achimenes flower the first year from rhizomes, cuttings or seeds.

Aeschynanthus   *Gesneriaceae*   Lipstick Plant
(formerly *Trichosporum*)

A fibrous-rooted epiphytic evergreen trailer with waxy leaves that remind of *Hoya bella,* flowers off and on throughout the year. Called lipstick plant because the red flower emerges weeks after the calyx has developed. *A. Lobbianus* has purplish stems to two feet long, fleshy leaves, brilliant red flowers in clusters; the one-inch calyx is blackish-purple, the hairy red flower is two inches long with blotches of yellow on the lower lobes. *A. pulcher* is similar to *A. Lobbianus* except the stems are green, calyx is green sometimes purple-tinged, the flowers are not hairy and are larger. *A. speciosa* has four-inch long orange and red flowers; if given short periods of water and dryness it can be had in flower most of the year.

Aglaonema modestum *(A. simplex)*   *Araceae*
                                                    Chinese Evergreen

A foliage plant that can exist with very little light. Under fluorescent light it flowers (insignificant) and forms clusters of bright red berries which have stayed on my plant for almost three years.

Day neutral, 6 inches, moderate, all purpose medium, moist. Propagate by stem cuttings.

Allamanda cathartica   *Apocynaceae*   Common
                                                              Alamanda

A clambering climber with whorled waxy leaves which handles easily as a pot plant with horizontal sprays. Golden yellow funnel-shaped flowers once a year last for about three months.

Day neutral, 4 to 6 inches, warm, all purpose medium kept moist while plant is growing but nearly dry while resting after flowering, extra fertilizer during entire growing period. Cut back to pot at end of rest period. Propagate by old or new wood cuttings.

Allophyton mexicanum   *Scrophulariaceae*   Mex-
                                                                  ican Foxglove

A perennial, crowded leaves on short stems, many half-inch long lavender flowers to a cluster, blooms on and off during the year.

Day neutral, 4 to 6 inches, moderate, humid, all purpose medium, moist. Propagate by seeds.

Alloplectus vittatus   *Gesneriaceae*

A Peruvian evergreen plant with silvery veins on velvety green leaves, yellow flowers with crimson calyx are enclosed in red bracts.

Gesneriad culture. Flowers first year from seeds or cuttings.

Alternanthera amoena   *Amaranthaceae*   Joseph's Coat

Small, branching bushy plants with leaves of many colors, like twisted coleus. Small white flowers most of the time.

Day neutral, 4 to 6 inches, warm, all purpose medium kept moist—plants wilt easily. Propagate by stem cuttings or root division.

Anthurium Scherzerianum   *Araceae*   Flamingo Flower

A small plant from a family of giants. Everblooming if the new roots along the aerial stems are kept covered with damp sphagnum. Flowers in all shades of red, pink, orange.

Day neutral, 6 inches, warm and humid, all purpose or epiphytic mix kept wet. Propagate by suckers, root cuttings, seeds.

Aphelandra squarrosa var. **Louisae**   *Acanthaceae*   Zebra Plant

Yellow flowers on square terminal spikes twice a year under lights. The white-veined shiny green foliage is always beautiful.

Plants tend to lose their bottom leaves, giving a leggy appearance. Semi-dry rest for a few weeks after the first blooming.

Day neutral, 2 to 3 inches, warm, all purpose medium kept
moist—when aphelandra runs out of water the foliage goes to
half-mast in a matter of minutes. Propagate by heel or tip cuttings. Start new plants from cuttings after the second flowering.

Araucaria excelsa   *Araucariaceae*   Norfolk
                                                          Island Pine

A permanent plant for many years without replacement or
cutting back, and tolerates diverse conditions. It grows cool or
warm, humid or dry, near or far from the tubes. Mine grows
about six inches a year with short internodes when placed
8 inches directly below the lamps. It is a charming miniature,
live Christmas tree whose light green growing tips are decora-
tion enough.

Day neutral, 6 to 12 inches, moderate, all purpose medium,
moist. Propagate by rooting the top leader of an old plant.
The side branches will root but they do not form a nicely
shaped tree.

Ardisia crispa   *Myrsinaceae*   Coral Berry
(A. crenulata, A. crenata)

This small tree stays under two feet in height with fluorescent
light culture. Shiny, leathery dark green leaves, flowers in its
second year, the fragrant white flowers followed by clusters
of bright red, waxy berries which endure on the plant for as
long as two years, or until the next flowering.

Day neutral, 5 to 6 inches, moderate (always under 75°), all
purpose medium kept evenly moist, mist the foliage frequently.

Propagate by tip cuttings. Seeds take six months or more to germinate.

Asparagus plumosus   *Liliaceae*   Asparagus
                                                              Fern

A graceful, feathery climbing or trailing plant with fleshy cordlike roots; tiny pinkish flowers in racemes once a year, followed by small bright red berries. I consider this a permanent plant in my fluorescent light garden.

Day neutral, 6 to 8 inches, moderate preferably not over 70°, all purpose medium, moist. Propagates easily by seeds, cuttings, or clump divisions.

Aucuba japonica var. variegata   *Cornaceae*   Gold
                                                             Dust Tree

An ornamental foliage plant with yellow-spotted leaves. Mature plant produces bright scarlet fruits that hang on for months, although by that time the plant may be too big and floppy to be allowed a place in a fluorescent light garden.

Day neutral, 6 to 8 inches, cool, all purpose medium, moist. Propagate by cuttings or seeds. Small rooted cuttings make the most satisfactory plants—just forget the uninteresting flowers.

Azalea hybrids   *Ericaceae*   Indian or Indica
                                                              Azalea

The florist's azaleas, as 'Albert and Elizabeth', require cool (35°-40°) temperature for several weeks before flowering. I have several plants that are kept in a coldframe until December or January, then brought into flower under fluorescent lights in my cool greenhouse. I bring one plant into the warm, humid plant room because I can't wait for the beautiful flowers; the plant flowers quickly and abundantly when forced in this manner, but the flowers last only a few days.

However, in my outdoor garden there are numerous hardy hybrid azaleas with flowers of intense and brilliant flame, orange and red colors. These azaleas are pruned as soon as they finish flowering in April and May, and by September multiple new budded growth has appeared from the pruned points. I take multi-branched cuttings in early October, root them with the bottom heat and high humidity of an electric propagating case, and by Christmas have small flower-laden plants growing happily under lights in the warm, humid plant factory. The buds which had formed on the plants outdoors swell and open as the cuttings root. This practice is contrary to what one is supposed to do with azaleas, but I have done it every year since I accidentally took an azalea cutting outdoors along with some other plants. I give these small 6- to 8-inch plants as gifts, and any still on hand in April are planted permanently outdoors.

Begonia   *Begoniaceae*

There is no beginning and no end to the begonias I have grown, do grow, and will grow in my fluorescent light gardens. Any word used to describe any other kind of plant may be applied to some sort of begonia: dependable, unreliable; untemperamental, quixotic; miniature, monstrous; upright, trailing; hairy, smooth; floriferous, shy; permanent, transient; beautiful, ug—but no, the antonym of beautiful cannot be applied to a begonia. Some are less beautiful than others, but there are no ugly ones. I have grown more than 200 species, varieties, and cultivars of begonias under fluorescent light, and I have yet to be disappointed.

For descriptive purposes, I prefer to classify begonias according to their root or stem structure, rather than according to foliage, although there is an inevitable overlapping.

TUBEROUS-ROOTED BEGONIAS. The summer-flowering tuberous begonias, including the tuberhybrida, multiflora, and pendula groups, whose magnificent flowers mock the rose, the carnation, the camellia and other flowers, will flower indoors under fluorescent light at any time of the year, and how welcome and appreciated they are in midwinter! Their cultural conditions are the same as described for *Sinningia speciosa* (florist's gloxinia), page 215, except that the begonias need 16 to 18 hours of light to flower. Pots of tuberous begonia plants that have flowered outdoors during the summer may be moved intact to an indoor fluorescent light garden where they will continue to flower for two to three months after short days and cool weather or frost would have terminated their growth outdoors. Cuttings can be taken from outdoor plants in August, rooted, potted, and flowered with the help of fluorescent light from November through about April. Note, however, that while tuberous begonias *flower* in long days, they *form tubers* in short days (about 8 hours of light and 16 hours of darkness). Thus plants grown from late-summer cuttings will flower with 16 to 18 hours of light but will not form tubers, and they will be exhausted and should be discarded after flowering. Late-summer cuttings can be taken for the purpose of providing the following year's outdoor plants if flowering is prevented and tuber formation is encouraged by means of short days and long nights from November to April. Several commercial growers "hold" summer-flowering begonia tubers under special conditions which allow the tubers to be purchased and potted in the fall.

Winter-flowering tuberous begonias ('Emily Clibran' is my

pet) require a temperature of 55 to 60 degrees. They are rather touchy plants, and I do not even try to grow them in the indoor fluorescent gardens. I keep them in the cool greenhouse where the fluorescent lights are automatically turned on when the outside weather is dull.

Semi-tuberous begonias (referred to as maple-leaf begonias) flower the year around in my plant factory. They look like little gnarled trees, and I use one or two when I feel the urge to build a replica of a garden in a tray.

RHIZOMATOUS BEGONIAS have a thick stem or rhizome from which the leaves, flowers and roots grow. The rhizome creeps on the top of the soil, not through it. Although many of the rhizomatous begonias are lusty, even gigantic plants, they are extremely shallow-rooted, and should be potted in shallow pots, preferably azalea-type pots. Most of the rex begonias are rhizomatous. Fluorescent light enhances and brings out the gorgeous colors in rex foliage. The rex begonias should be placed about 12 to 16 inches below the lamps—placed too close, the colors tend to bleach. This is true also of *Begonia masoniana* (iron cross)—though not a rex begonia, its emerald green and mahogany leaves fade in too-bright light. The rex begonias and *B. masoniana* flower quite monotonously at 16 inches below the lamps. I would love them if they did not flower—there is enough glory in the stunning foliage. Rhizomatous begonias grown in natural light usually have a dormant period in winter; they may stop growing and a few sorts may lose their foliage altogether and appear to be dead. This dormancy does not occur for me with fluorescent light culture.

FIBROUS-ROOTED BEGONIAS fall into four groups; semperflorens, cane-stemmed, small-leaved branching, and hirsute. *Semperflorens* (wax) begonias are quite without shame when grown with 14 to 16 hours of fluorescent light. They can be as close as 6 inches from the lamps or as far away as 12 inches. The semi-double and double flowering hybrids produce a seemingly endless succession of flowers. I usually keep wax begonias pinched back in bushy clumps, but I also, contrary to the rules of semperflorens begonia culture, allow some plants to grow long sprays which become hanging plants when the weight of the flowers pulls the stems down.

The *cane-stemmed begonias*—the angel wings—seem to flower unceasingly under fluorescent lights, also. True, many of the angel wings are by nature just too big and sprawly for a small indoor garden. And an angel wing begonia is unusually sensitive to a draft—if you find some morning that you have a long cane with only a silly little tassel of leaves at the end, you can be fairly sure a draft of air has hit the plant. If you can be patient, the leaves will grow back; if not, cut the cane off at a node close to the pot and new sprouts will soon appear. Some small angel wing begonias which are an everlasting part of my fluorescent light gardens are: 'Dainty Spray', 'Elaine', 'May Queen', 'Pinafore', 'Orange Rubra' (I grow this one next to Streptocarpus 'Constant Nymph' because I love the visual color combination of salmon-orange and blue).

Of the many *small-leaved branching begonias* I have grown, I have selected 'Dancing Girl', the arching, drooping 'Mme. Fanny Giron' that says Merry Christmas all the time, 'Preussen', 'Catalina', 'Digswelliana', and 'It' to be permanent residents in my fluorescent light gardens, because the foliage is delightful and the plants are rarely without flowers.

The *hirsute* (hairy) *begonias* require less humidity than the others, and grow and flower quite well with a relative humidity of 35 to 40 per cent, although they do magnificently with the higher relative humidity of 50 to 60 per cent. They will not tolerate overwatering, however. Begonia 'General Jacques' (B.

'San Miguel') is not only my favorite hirsute begonia, it is the most cherished plant of all that I grow in my fluorescent light gardens. If (a thought too appalling to contemplate) I should be restricted to just one indoor plant, my choice would be Begonia 'San Miguel'.

On the first cool fall evenings our local television weather forecaster can be depended upon to say, "Better bring in the begonias, mother." Indeed you should bring them indoors— straight to your fluorescent light garden. Every indoor garden should have begonias.

Beloperone guttata   *Acanthaceae*   Shrimp Plant

Showy, overlapping shrimp-colored bracts beneath small white flowers in drooping terminal spikes, the year around. Blooms first year from cuttings. Prune frequently. A horticultural form, 'Yellow Queen', has golden or chartreuse bracts and is more dwarf and floriferous than *B. guttata*.

Day neutral, 3 to 4 inches, warm, all purpose medium, moist. Propagate by cuttings.

Bertolonia   *Melastomaceae*

Dwarf creeping stems, leaves purplish underneath and various metallic colors above. *B. maculata* and *B. pubescens* are both good in a terrarium under fluorescent light.

Day neutral, 9 to 10 inches, warm and humid, all purpose medium kept moist. Propagate by stem cuttings over heat, or seeds.

Boea hygroscopica   *Gesneriaceae*

A 6-inch tall plant with bright yellow-centered vivid blue flowers that are flat with short tubes like Saintpaulia, pleated bright green leaves. The fruit is spirally twisted like streptocarpus.

Gesneriad culture. It likes a daily watering. Propagate by division of the crown or seeds.

Browallia speciosa (B. major)   *Solanaceae*

An annual; blue flowers all year. Pinch back for a bushy pot plant or let trail over edge of bench. Start new plants from cuttings or seed once a year.

Day neutral, 3 to 4 inches, warm, all purpose medium, moist.

Buxus microphylla var. *japonica*   *Buxaceae*   Box, Boxwood

A slow-growing boxwood with small shiny leaves, plump shrubby shape.

Day neutral, 6 inches, cool, all purpose medium, moist. Propagate by stem cuttings, or by division of the plant.

Cactus   *Cactaceae*

I know no better definition of a succulent plant than that in *Hortus Second:* "A succulent plant, or a succulent, is strictly one that is full of sap; but in horticultural usage it is a thick fleshy plant, and such plants are commonly juicy or sappy. For the most part, succulent plants are native in regions that are arid or semi-arid for at least part of the year, and the succulence has relation to water storage."

The *Cactaceae* is the largest plant family of which all the species are succulent, but succulent plants are found in a number of other plant families.

The fluorescent light gardener who is unable or unwilling to provide the relative humidity usually required by tropical plants when they are grown indoors, the beginning gardener who has never grown any kind of plant indoors, the busy gardener who can tend plants perhaps only once in every week or ten days . . . these people will find cacti and some other succulents the ideal plants for growing under their household conditions.

Cactus nomenclature is intricate, overlapping, confused, and in a state of reclassification. I am very particular about having a label in or on every plant in my possession (all right, there are a few that read, "What is this?"), but I have just about given up on trying to keep my cactus plants identified correctly. In any event, it is their place of origin that dictates their culture. I handle cacti according to which of two types they may be: those that grow in desert regions and have adapted to their surroundings; and those that live in less arid regions, the epiphytic cacti.

The desert-type cacti are the patient ones that will thank you to ignore them for days at a time and direct your tender, loving care to some other plant. I have more than fifty different desert-type cacti in fluorescent light gardens. The tallest reaches 6 inches and the largest is in a 4-inch pot.

Desert cacti cannot tolerate water around their roots. The physical condition of the potting medium is really more important than its chemical content. The potting medium must be open, so that water drains through swiftly. Sand alone is not a good potting medium for cacti. The majority of the desert

cacti will grow well in sand and loam mixed in such proportions as make a good, open compost. Generally, a cactus medium
should be slightly on the alkaline side (pH 7.1 or 7.2), rather
than neutral or slightly acid.

Cacti do not grow rapidly and do not require the stimulant
of chemical fertilizers. A slow-acting organic fertilizer, such as
bone meal, is useful and may be added to a batch of cactus
potting medium. Fresh organic fertilizers such as manure
should not be given to desert cacti. The size of pot should be
such that the spines are within the width of the pot rim.

The plants can almost touch the lamps, which should burn
14 to 16 hours a day. Desert cacti should be watered no oftener
than once a week. Apply the water around the plant, not over
the top.

The foregoing recommendations are for cacti growing in
conditions that simulate a desert, to the degree possible indoors
—dry air and strong light from fluorescent lamps.

But . . . remember the stories you have read and the pictures you have seen of cactus plants with flowers often bigger
than the plants themselves? In nature, the desert cacti grow
some distance apart. The water supply for a large part of the
year is restricted and the dry soil will not support a dense
vegetation. But when the rains come, as they eventually do
to warm deserts, the cacti respond to the greater amount of
moisture by growing and flowering. They respond in the same
way when grown under fluorescent lights in the same humid
atmosphere that is good for begonias and gesneriads. Most of
my cactus plants are placed right in among the tropical plants
in my plant factory. They are watered infrequently, they are
not chemically fertilized, but they love the moist atmosphere
of about 50 per cent relative humidity.

I may very well come to regret keeping my cactus plants in
a growing state the year around, in contrariness to the advice

of expert cactus growers who say that the plants have a dormancy requirement which must be observed. My oldest cactus plants are about five years old—they have done just fine with year-round culture thus far but it is not impossible that they will be shorter lived, as cacti go, than if I gave them a long winter rest.

A few of my desert cacti are: *Cereus Pringlei (Pachycereus Pringlei); Echinocactus Grusonii (Ferocactus Grusonii),* golden barrel cactus; *Gymnocalycium,* barrel cactus; *Lemaireocereus marginatus,* organ pipe cactus; *Mammillaria bocasana,* powder puff cactus; *Mammillaria elegans,* pincushion cactus; *Mammillaria rhodantha; Notocactus,* ball cactus; *Opuntia,* prickly pear or bunny ears cactus; *Parodia aureispina,* Tom Thumb cactus; *Rebutia,* crown cactus.

The culture of succulent plants of families other than *Cactaceae* is similar to that of desert cactus. All succulents, no matter what plant family they belong to, want well-drained soil, good ventilation, water at the correct time, and good light. Plants of a succulent nature are so designated in this alphabetical listing of plants.

Caladium   *Araceae*

A tuberous-rooted plant that grows seven or eight months before dormancy. The myriad colors, patterns and leaf shapes of the varieties of *C. bicolor* get fancier and prettier every year. *C. Humboldtii* is a small species requiring more humidity than the hybrids. Remove the dull, spathe-enclosed flowers as they appear so all the tuber's energy will go into producing the beautiful leaves.

Day neutral, 2 to 12 inches, warm—grows best at 75° to 80°, all purpose acid medium, moist. Propagate by seeds.

Calathea   *Marantaceae*

Commonly but incorrectly known as marantas, these richly colored and intricately patterned tropical foliage plants flower reluctantly, but the foliage is preferred to the flowers. *C. micans* is a miniature; *C. argyraea, insignis, zebrina* are larger but all are easily managed in a fluorescent light garden.

Day neutral, 4 to 6 inches, moderate, very loose all purpose medium, lots of water and frequent washing to prevent red spider, fertilize heavily for best colors. Propagate by crown division, tubers, or cuttings.

Callistemon viminalis   *Myrtaceae*   Bottle Brush

A tree of pendulous habit with showy red flowers in dense spikes. Can be grown for about a year in an indoor garden, then is too big to handle and should be moved to a greenhouse or planted outdoors in a warm region.

Day neutral, 6 to 8 inches, moderate, all purpose medium, moist. Propagate by seeds.

Campanula   *Campanulaceae*   Italian Bellflower,
                                            Falling Stars

Starlike saucer shaped flowers on dainty trailing stems. I handle as a pot plant by pinching the trailers short. *C. isophylla* has blue flowers and *C. isophylla* var. *alba* has white flowers.

Day neutral, 3 to 4 inches, moderate, light all purpose slightly alkaline medium, moist. Cut plant back to base of branches after flowering, keep under the lights but water sparingly for 5 to 8 weeks. When plant starts growing again resume watering and fertilizing and pinch out branch tips to encourage more flowering stems. Remove faded flowers so plant will not use its energy to set seeds.

Carissa grandiflora var. *nana compacta*   *Apocynaceae*
Natal Plum

Very slow-growing, low, dense plant with round overlapping, exceedingly shiny leaves, fragrant white flowers off and on during the year. The scarlet fruit is outlandishly large for the small plant. A real delight, and a plant to be cherished.

Day neutral, 6 to 8 inches, warm, all-purpose medium, moist, spray the leaves frequently. Propagate by cuttings.

Ceropegia   *Asclepiadaceae*

Not strictly succulents, but with a tendency to succulence, these climbing or trailing diminutive plants with threadlike stems thrive in several different locations in my fluorescent light gardens. I place some on top of the fixtures and the trailing stems make a lacy curtain as they fall straight down past the lamps. Others I train round and round small spiral earring stands. The minuscule flowers remind me of the balloon in ads for Jules Verne's "Around the World in 80 Days." I have never grown a ceropegia in a pot larger than two inches. Recommended: *C. Barklyi* (umbrella plant); *C. debilis; C. Woodii* (rosary vine, heart vine).

Day neutral, 4 to 6 inches, moderate, to 60% relative humidity, a sandy all purpose medium which may be allowed to dry out. Propagated by cuttings, tiny tubers, seeds.

Chirita   *Gesneriaceae*   Hindustan Gentian

Pot plants from the mountains of India. *C. asperifolia* (formerly *C. Blumei)* is a bushy, erect plant 1 to 1½ feet tall, vivid purple tubular flowers with white faces over a long period. *C. lavandulacea* is best treated as an annual and started from seed or cuttings every year. *C. sinensis,* the Chinese chirita, is a low-growing rosette form with bright green leaves conspicuously marked with a network of silver; shy about flowering but does produce its disappointing pale lilac flowers if plant is placed very close to lamps; plant is very durable and evergreen, and the foliage is exceptionally beautiful.

Gesneriad culture. Plants need water almost every day. Propagate by seeds or leaf cuttings.

Chlorophytum   *Liliaceae*   Spider Plant

A proliferous, undemanding hanging plant whose offshoots look to me more like the rays of a Roman candle than like spiders. Stands neglect for days on end, produces long growths with small purplish flowers in racemes at the ends. New plants, which will root in any damp place they touch, are formed following the flowers. It's an ordinary, old-fashioned plant, but I would not be without its quiet activity in my fluorescent light gardens. Recommended: *C. bichetii* (I have not been able to verify this name) is a miniature with 6-inch grass-like leaves with cream-white stripes along the edges and occasionally in the middle; *C. capense (elatum)* is larger and has the ivory-white stripe in the middle of the leaf.

Day neutral, 8 to 10 inches, moderate, all purpose medium, preferably kept moist but tolerates drying out. Propagate by dividing plant or by potting up the plantlets.

Chrysothemis   *Gesneriaceae*

Fleshy plants that stay about 8 inches tall under lights. *C. Friedrichsthaliana* has bright green leaves, yellow flowers with orange spots, green or yellow calyx. *C. pulchella* is similar except foliage has a coppery glow and the flowers are larger with an orangish calyx in contrast to the yellow flowers.

Culture as for *Sinningia speciosa*. Propagate by seeds or cuttings.

Cissus   *Vitaceae*

Mostly tendril-climbing vines with your choice of small, medium or large leaves. Recommended: *C. rhombifolia,* grape ivy; *C. striata,* the miniature grape ivy; *C. antartica,* kangaroo ivy. *C. quadrangularis* is an odd succulent with rich green four-winged stems, often almost leafless and looking like a spineless cactus, but it climbs and produces green flowers and red berries.

Day neutral, may be allowed to twine around a fluorescent lamp or grow as much as 8 to 10 inches from the lamp, moderate temperature, 60% humidity, all purpose medium kept moist. Propagate by cuttings.

Citrus   *Rutaceae*

Miniature citrus trees—those that are naturally dwarf or grow slowly—are unendingly delightful in a fluorescent light garden, grow for years in 3- to 6-inch pots, and seem to be always busy flowering and fruiting. Recommended: *C. aurantifolia* (acid lime) is spiny, has small leaves and tart, thin-skinned green fruit. *C. Limonia* var. *ponderosa* (ponderosa lemon) sharp spines, fragrant flowers, heavy pear-shaped lemons at intervals. *C. mitis* (calamondin orange) has flowers and green and ripe tiny oranges practically the year around in the fluorescent light garden in my living room fireplace.

Day neutral, 4 to 6 inches, cool to moderate, loamy all purpose medium kept moist to slightly dry, 60% humidity, no sudden temperature changes, fertilize sparingly. Hand pollinate for fruit, except *C. mitis* which, at least for me, is self-pollinating. Propagate by cuttings.

Clematis   *Ranunculaceae*   Virgins Bower

I have flowered several hybrids of the Jackmanii type (the only one of the three types of clematis that flowers on current growth) under fluorescent lights. Having been advised that clematis must have a cool root run, I potted the plants (purchased from a clematis specialist) in 6-inch standard clay pots, and put a trellis in each pot. The pots were placed in insulated ice buckets with crumpled newspaper wadded between pot and the wall of the bucket. The newspaper was kept wet, making a crude evaporative cooling system, and by golly the plants flowered in the otherwise tropical atmosphere of the plant factory.

Day neutral, 4 to 6 inches, slightly alkaline all purpose soil. Having proven to myself that it could be done, and not caring to devote the special attention again, my plants were moved outdoors, where they have done well for the three years since their indoor treatment.

Clivia miniata   *Amaryllidaceae*   Kafir Lily

A strap-leaved evergreen plant that requires an inordinate amount of space but more than pays its rent when it flowers. My six-year-old plant is in an 11-quart plastic household bucket and it produces two spikes of fluorescent orange amaryllis-like flowers each year, both at the same time, I should add. I move it to the greenhouse in the summertime and bring it to the indoor fluorescent light garden when I spy the buds pushing out between the heavy leaves, usually in November. Cool culture is usually recommended for clivia, but it flowers magnificently in the tropical plant room for me.

Day neutral, plant almost touching lamps, all purpose medium kept moist while plant is budding and flowering. Do not move clivia from pot to pot until it forces you to do so when the roots burst the pot.

Codiaeum variegatum   *Euphorbiaceae*   Croton

The extensively variable, colorful ornamental foliage makes crotons wonderful subjects for fluorescent light gardens. I know of no naturally small crotons, but the large ones are kept in hand by pruning once a year. I have never seen the small flowers, but am satisfied with the foliage, which may range from green to a brilliant shrimp color on the same plant at the same time.

Day neutral, 4 to 6 inches, warm, high humidity, all purpose medium, moist. Propagate by cuttings of half-ripened wood over bottom heat.

Codonanthe   *Gesneriaceae*   Central
American Bellflower

Evergreen fibrous-rooted climbers or creepers in flower almost continuously. *C. crassifolia* has shiny leaves with tiny red spots scattered on the under side—I tried to remove the spots on my first plant, thinking they were insects. The waxy white flowers are red-splotched inside the tube. *C. crassifolia* 'Panama' is similar but has darker green leaves. I also grow an unidentified species that produces tiny yellow tubular flowers almost continuously.

Gesneriad culture. Codonanthe likes copious watering. Propagate by cuttings, seeds.

Coffea arabica *Rubiaceae* Common
or Arabian Coffee

An evergreen, quick growing plant with shiny dark green leaves. My three-year-old plant from a seed has not flowered, but I anticipate the fragrant, pure white ¾-inch long flowers. It is a delightful 10-inch tall plant in a 4-inch pot.

Day neutral, 4 to 6 inches, moderate, all purpose medium, moist. Probably I have not yet found the right combination of dark and light periods and temperature for this plant. Propagate by seeds.

Coleus Blumei *Labiatae*

The good old dependable standby whose beautiful foliage is enhanced a hundred times under fluorescent lights.

Day neutral, 4 to 6 inches, moderate to warm, all purpose medium, moist. Plants wilt easily. Propagate by cuttings of favorites, or by seed any time of the year. Pinch the plants ruthlessly and always remove the flowers as soon as they appear, to prevent seed from setting.

Collinia elegans *Palmaceae* Dwarf Palm
(Chamaedorea elegans; Neanthe bella)

Soft, graceful, clustered palm often found in dish gardens. My 8- to 10-inch tall plants grow in 2-inch pots. I did not recognize the tiny yellow, pinhead-size flowers as flowers the first time I saw them, but now I take a particular delight in looking for the flowers.

Day neutral, 5 to 8 inches, warm, all purpose medium, moist, best when 60% humidity can be provided.

Columnea   *Gesneriaceae*   Goldfish Plant

Trailing or upright plants from Central America. The 1963 Gesneriad Register lists 113 species and hybrids now in cultivation. I have grown more than 75 different columneas in my fluorescent light gardens, and flowered almost all of them. 'College Bred Columneas' is a group name for individually named hybrids produced at Cornell University. All in the group are fine for fluorescent light culture. Especially good are C. 'Ithacan' and C. 'Othello' which are almost everblooming for me. C. 'V. Covert' is a branching upright plant with small pinkish red flowers almost continuously. Of the species, I like *C. arguta,* orange-red 2-inch long flowers; *C. gloriosa,* 3-inch vivid red flowers; *C. hirta,* bright green soft hairy leaves and a multitude of orange-scarlet flowers that look like goldfish swimming in midair; *C. microphylla,* tiny leaves giving a fern-like appearance to a trailing plant loaded with red and lemon-yellow flowers; *C. minor* (formerly *Trichantha minor*), which will twine its widely spaced unequal leaf pairs around a string or chain and produce dark purple tubular flowers with yellow faces; *C. tulae* cv. 'Flava', small vivid yellow flowers throughout the year.

Gesneriad culture, flowers first year from cuttings or seeds.

Crassula   *Crassulaceae*

Almost any of the thirty or more species and hybrids of these succulent plants available from specialists are good under fluorescent lights, although young plants rarely flower. Recommended: *C. argentea* (jade plant), thick shiny foliage and rosy-red flowers; *C. falcata* (scarlet paintbrush), flattened curved gray-green leaves arranged like parallel shingles and crimson flowers; *C. marginalis,* prostrate succulent for baskets, tiny, rounded, grayish-green leaves with red spots on margin, reddish tinged flowers; *C. perforata* (string of buttons); *C. perfossa* (necklace vine).

Succulent culture.

Crossandra infundibuliformis   *Acanthaceae*
(C. undulaefolia)

I always want to call this plant an orange jasmine but there is no relationship, and I had better not add another incorrect name to horticultural literature. Leaves are shiny dark green and flowers are orange in an angled spike, and I love the plant because it flowers on and on.

Day neutral, 3 to 4 inches, warm, high humidity, all purpose medium, moist. Propagate by cuttings over bottom heat. Seeds are available, but I have found them slow and uncertain to germinate. Try to get a cutting from a friend, or buy a small plant.

Cryptanthus   *Bromeliaceae*   Earth Stars

Low flat rosettes of stiff leaves prickly on the edges and always unusually colored. Will grow in a pot, or in the air as the epiphytes they really are. They withstand neglect, and should not be disturbed for several years once potted. Recommended: *C. Beuckeri, C. bivittatus,* in fact any of the species or hybrids available from specialists.

Day neutral, 6 to 8 inches, warm, humusy medium, good drainage, grow dry like cacti. Propagate by offsets which appear frequently on pot-grown plants, or by a basal leaf pulled from stem.

× *Cryptbergia Meadii*   *Bromeliaceae*

Everything said about cryptanthus applies to cryptbergia, which is an intergeneric hybrid between billbergia and cryptanthus.

Cyanotis   *Commelinaceae*

Succulent creeping or trailing relatives of the inch plant. Recommended: *C. kewensis,* teddy-bear plant; *C. somaliensis,* pussy ears.

Day neutral, 4 to 6 inches, warm, lots of fresh air, all purpose medium kept on the dry side. Propagate by cuttings.

Cymbalaria muralis   *Scrophulariaceae*   Kenilworth Ivy

No two ways about it, this is a weed, and it will pop up in every potted plant, like greenhouse oxalis does, unless you heartlessly pull it out when you spot it where it is not wanted. Nevertheless, it is a dainty creeping or trailing plant with tiny lavender flowers the year around, charming trained on a wire sphere. No cultural instructions are needed—it grows in any conditions above freezing and sets seed wickedly.

Cyperus alternifolius   *Cyperaceae*   Umbrella
                                                  Plant

Sort of weedy looking and not very pretty, but I grew it once from seed out of curiosity. My batch of plants did equally well in pots standing in water and in pots not in water in which the all purpose medium was kept constantly wet. I banished the plants to the outdoor pool when they reached a foot in height.

Desmodium motorium (D. gyrans)   *Leguminosae*
                                          Telegraph Plant

A curiosity I was happy to grow just once, from seed, in my fluorescent light garden. In the light and in a temperature of 72° or above, the lateral leaves move jerkily up, down and sideways, as if involved in confused semaphore. Fun but spooky. Has 1/4-inch long purple flowers, seed pods to 1 1/2 inches long.

Day neutral, 4 to 6 inches, warm all purpose medium, moist. Treat as an annual.

Diastema   *Gesneriaceae*

Lush green leaves, miniature flowers, on a small plant that grows from scaly rhizomes and flowers for five to six months before going dormant. *D. quinquevulnerum* has many white flowers; *D. vexans,* white flowers with purple marks; and there is a compact, blue-flowering species with dark, metallic green leaves, *D. maculata.*

Culture same as achimenes. Propagate by cuttings, rhizomes.

Dieffenbachia   *Araceae*   Dumb Cane,
                                                            Mother-in-law Plant

One of the toughest of indoor foliage plants, except that it
will lose leaves and die if left for any length of time in a temperature under 50°. *D. picta* runs into many forms of spotted
and mottled green and white leaves. The plants often grow 2
to 3 feet in height, and stop developing good leaves. At this
point, they should be topped, the tops rooted and the canes
cut into 2-inch pieces and put in sand where they will produce
shoots that will root and form new plants.

Day neutral, 8 to 10 inches, warm, all purpose medium,
moist.

Dionaea muscipula   *Droseraceae*   Venus
                                                              Fly Trap

A little bug-eating plant of which I want no more than one.
One of nature's wonders, I'm sure, but too predatory for my
liking. Pot in sphagnum and set the pot in about an inch of
water, or keep the sphagnum very wet. Keep it cool and humid
in a terrarium under fluorescent lights.

Dizygotheca elegantissima   *Araliaceae*   False
(Aralia elegantissima)   Aralia, Finger Aralia

An airily graceful palmlike plant that provides a pleasant
contrast to the heavy foliage of most tropical plants. Can be
grown under lights while a juvenile—up to about two years—
but will eventually grow too tall to manage, unless you cut it
back and root prune once a year.

Day neutral, 8 to 10 inches, warm, sandy all purpose medium, moist. Loses lower leaves if deprived of light and 65 to 70 per cent humidity. This species does not branch but a several-stemmed plant is obtained by cutting the main stem close to the pot or by planting several rooted cuttings together in a clump.

Dracaena Godseffiana   *Liliceae*   Dracena

A small, slow-growing tropical foliage shrub with glassy, leathery leaves splotched hit-or-miss with white. *D. Godseffiana* 'Florida Beauty' is a dwarf plant with yellow splotches on the leaves.

Day neutral, 4 to 6 inches, warm, all purpose medium, moist to wet. Propagate by tip cuttings or pieces of stem with several nodes.

Dyckia rariflora   *Bromeliaceae*

A tiny plant with stiff sprays of spiny-edged leaves and tall spikes of orange or yellow flowers.

Day neutral, 2 inches, moderate, all purpose medium kept on the dry side. Propagate by the offshoots.

Echeveria   *Crassulaceae*

American succulents with broad leaves in rosettes and flowers in spikes, racemes, or panicles. *E. agavoides,* starlike rosette with rigid fleshy triangular pointed leaves of glossy pale apple green, leaf margins frequently reddish, spine tipped. *E. elegans,* a dense rosette of narrow pointed, fleshy, concave light green leaves, upper half rich crimson red. *E. gibbiflora* var. *metallica,* large spoonshaped bronzy-amethyst leaves with metallic luster and translucent margins. *E. glauca,* open rosette with numerous runners, blue-green red-tipped leaves.

Succulent culture.

Episcia *Gesneriaceae* Peacock Foliage Plant

Evergreen fibrous-rooted trailing plants, probably next in popularity to the African violet as a gesneriad house plant. Flowers are white, blue, red, orange, yellow, and pink but the beautifully marked decorative leaves are the real attraction. The 1963 Gesneriad Register lists 150 names. There is a difference of opinion among episcia growers as to the amount of fluorescent light the plants need. Some growers say full light, like gloxinias. In my experience, the episcias will not tolerate strong light—with it, they develop twisted, deformed centers. Mine are grown under the extreme ends of the lamps and at the outer edges of the growing areas. Occasionally I wrap two or three layers of cheesecloth or nylon netting around the lamps to filter the light.

Day neutral, 10 to 12 inches, warm (NEVER below 55°), all purpose medium, moist. Propagate by runners or seeds.

Eucnide bartoniodes *Loasaceae* Golden Tassel

A beautiful little plant that I found listed in Park Seed Co. catalog as "Microsperma Golden Tassel." Neither Mr. Park nor I are sure whether it is an eucnide or a mentzelia, but *Eucnide bartoniodes* is also called *Mentzelia gronoviaefolia,* so we are probably close in our identification. It is an American annual herb, 5 to 6 inches in height under lights, with bright yellow flowers centered with a feathery cluster of golden stamens. It flowers indefinitely and is self-pollinating.

Day neutral, 4 to 6 inches, moderate, all purpose medium, moist. Propagate by seeds or cuttings.

Euphorbia   *Euphorbiaceae*

A large group of more or less succulent plants and small trees, sometimes cactus-like, all with a milky juice that is capable of producing a dermititis similar to that of poison ivy on susceptible individuals. Almost all euphorbias are good subjects for fluorescent light gardens except the unmanageable large sorts. *E. splendens (E. Milii)* is the familiar crown of thorns and almost always has at least a few flowers; it is usual for *E. splendens* to lose and replace a few leaves with monotonous regularity. *E. submammillaris,* corn cob, is a spiny plant with minute purple bracts. *E. pulcherrima,* the poinsettia, is not a subject for a day neutral fluorescent light garden because it flowers in short days that must be accurately timed.

Succulent culture. Propagate by cuttings.

Exacum affine   *Gentianaceae*   German Violet

Just about the sweetest little thing, in fragrance and appearance, that one can have in a fluorescent light garden. A biennial with small gentian-blue flowers in abundance and small shiny green leaves. I start plants from seed once a year, and grow them in 2½-inch pots.

Day neutral, 6 to 8 inches, moderate to cool, all purpose medium kept moist. Propagate by seeds.

✕ *Fatshedera Lizei*   *Araliaceae*   Tree Ivy
French Ivy

An intergeneric hybrid between *Fatsia japonica* and *Hedera Helix,* this is a foliage plant with vining characteristics, not self-supporting. Mine is fastened where needed with plastic plant ties to a length of white metal picket fencing which is hung from the ceiling. The plant has low light requirements and receives sufficient reflected light from the fluorescent lights in the plant factory. Mine has grown up its improvised trellis and started across the ceiling.

Fatsia japonica   *Araliaceae*   Aralia

A slow-growing large leaved plant that tolerates low light and lack of attention. The leaves have a particular affinity for dust and should be washed regularly. Grow it anyplace where it will receive a little reflected light and where you can accommodate its size.

Ferns

You may not believe it until you see it, but it is possible to have too bloomin' many blooms in a fluorescent light garden. When a bench or garden becomes such a kaleidoscope that I cannot see the individual beauty of a single plant or flower, I separate the riotously flowering plants from one another with ferns. I do not have a separate fern garden, but there are always a dozen or so pots of ferns growing on the benches in the plant factory. I also use the ferns as grace notes in the small gardens which are spotted all around the house.

Gordon Foster, Maplewood, New Jersey, has extensive indoor

fern gardens under fluorescent lights. For several years he successfully used a one-to-one combination of cool white and warm
white fluorescent lamps, now uses all Gro-Lux lamps for the
tropical ferns that are adaptable to continuous growth all year.
The lights burn 14 hours a day and are suspended 18 to 24
inches above the tables. Some of the taller species reach the
lights at times. The daytime temperature in the fernery ranges
from 72° to 85°, dropping during the dark period to 60° to
65°. Mr. Foster emphasizes that there must be a lower night
temperature for successful fern growing. Fern spores germinate
readily under the lights; in fact, Mr. Foster finds volunteers
in his benches rather often. Generally, the tropical ferns like
a humid climate, and for their growing medium, a loose, moist
woodland mulch with pebbles added.

Mr. Foster has a definite preference for clay pots for most
ferns, and finds that the tub or squatty type pot (wider than
deep) is best for these shallow-rooted plants. He makes "log
cabin" baskets or cribs of long-lasting redwood for his epiphytic species. By lining the baskets with osmundine fiber,
humus, and chopped fir bark, proper drainage and ventilation
so necessary for these tree-loving sorts are assured.

Mr. Foster suggests these tropical ferns as being especially
good in a fluorescent light garden: *Adiantum Capillus-Veneris*
(Southern maidenhair or Venushair fern); *Adiantum hispidu-
lum* (rosy maidenhair fern); *Cyrtomium falcatum* (Japanese
holly fern); *Polystichum tsus-simense* (Tsus-sima holly fern),
good in a terrarium or on a bench; *Davallia fejeensis* var. *plu-
mosa,* an epiphytic fern with fuzzy rhizomes.

Ficus   *Moraceae*   Creeping Fig

The Indian rubber plant, *F. elastica,* belongs to this family, but I know no reason to have it in the house, let alone in a fluorescent garden. Two delights are *F. pumila* var. *minima* (*F. repans*), tiny crinkled heart-shape leaves of dark green—the most beautiful use I have seen is in Mrs. William Prescott's Long Island kitchen, where the plant clambers upon and clings to a white stone wall (one couldn't buy wallpaper so pretty). *F. radicans* var. *variegata* has slim pointed silvery green leaves marked with creamy white. I grow both species in terrariums under lights.

Day neutral, 10 to 12 inches, warm, all purpose medium kept moist. Propagate by cuttings of the rooting stems.

Fittonia Verschaffeltii   *Acanthaceae*   Nerve
                                                          Plant, Mosaic Plant

Low, creeping foliage plants with dark green leaves and deep red veins. The variety *argyoneura* is veined with white and silver; variety *Pearcei* is light green veined with pink. Truly, fittonia foliage is lush and beautiful, and it has surprised me by flowering in the fluorescent light garden. Reluctantly, I have banned it from the premises—I cannot stand slugs, and fittonia and slugs are synonymous in my mind.

Day neutral, 10 to 12 inches, warm (never below 55°), humid, all purpose medium kept moist.

Propagate by cuttings.

Fuchsia hybrids   *Onagraceae*

Generally, fuchsias need a night temperature below 65° to set buds. I have not grown any of the fuchsia species under lights, but have found some vigorous and beautiful hybrids that go on flowering for months when grown side by side with the gloxinias and begonias. The trick, apparently, is to start with cuttings which are rooted in warmth and potted several cuttings to a pot. Plants started in warmth usually continue to grow and flower in the tropical atmosphere. Two especially good hybrids for me are 'Brigadoon' and 'Swingtime'.

Day neutral, 4 to 6 inches, moderate, all purpose medium kept moist. Propagate by cuttings, seeds.

Geogenanthus undatus   *Commelinaceae*   Seer-
(formerly *Dichorisandra mosaica undata*)   sucker Plant

Crinkled, leathery valentine-shaped leaves olive green with purple backs. Grows compact and low with fluorescent light culture.

Day neutral, 8 to 10 inches, moderate, all purpose medium, moist.

Gesneriads   *Gesneriaceae*

Probably the most rewarding flowering plants one can grow in a fluorescent light garden are the gesneriads. There are thousands of varieties of African violets in cultivation and hundreds of their exotic relatives available to the indoor gardener from nurserymen who specialize in gesneriads. Hybridizing the gesneriads is becoming a popular American indoor sport. Interspecific and intergeneric hybrids of great beauty have been produced by amateur growers in fluorescent light gardens in basements.

The gesneriads include tuberous-rooted plants (like *Sinningia,* including the gloxinia of horticulture or florist's gloxinia), rhizomatous-rooted plants (like *Achimenes, Kohleria, Smithiantha*), and fibrous-rooted plants (like *Saintpaulia, Columnea, Episcia, Streptocarpus, Aeschynanthus*). A tuberous- or rhizomatous-rooted gesneriad requires a period of dormancy after flowering. The fibrous-rooted plants, with a few exceptions, grow the year around.

Most of the gesneriads now in cultivation, except possibly the Alpine species that require lower temperatures than are usually possible in a home, will grow under artificial light, and nearly all will flower. A few, like *Rechsteineria Warszewiczii*, are by nature tall and awkward plants hardly worth the space and effort required to keep raising the lights high enough to accommodate them.

The gesneriads are mostly day-neutral plants, that is, they do not require a precise number of hours of light and dark to flower. Exceptions seem to be some columneas, some achimenes, and occasionally one species of a genus in which the other known species and hybrids do well under lights. An example of the last is *Streptocarpus saxorum*—I have never flowered it with 14 to 16 hours of light, nor do I know anyone who has, yet it flowers almost continuously in my greenhouse.

The conditions which should prevail for most of the gesneriads are 14 to 16 continuous hours of light in each 24 hours, a distance of 4 to 8 inches between top of plant and tubes, a night temperature of 62 degrees, a day temperature of 72 to 80 degrees, a relative humidity of 50 to 55 per cent, a very porous well-drained potting medium, good circulation of air around the plants but no direct drafts, regular fertilizing while plants are in growth, watering frequently enough to keep the planting medium moist but not soggy, prompt removal of fading flowers and deteriorating foliage, and ideally there should be enough space so that the plants do not touch each other. The various genera of the *Gesneriaceae* are listed in alphabetical order.

Gossypium   *Malvaceae*   Cotton

I do not know the correct name of the cotton plants I grow every year from seeds purchased under the name of "Ornamental Cotton." The bushy plants go to about 18 inches in height, bear pink buds, creamy flowers, and big white cotton bolls in a display that continues for about six months. Children can't quite believe their eyes when they are allowed to pluck a cotton boll from the plant.

Day neutral, 4 to 6 inches, moderate, all purpose medium, moist. Discard this annual plant when it stops budding, although I have held on to one for three months beyond this time, just to have a plant for young cotton-picking guests.

Gesneria cuneifolia   *Gesneriaceae*

A small, evergreen fibrous-rooted nearly stemless plant with a rosette of narrow, four-inch long, toothed, shiny green leaves and bright red tubular flowers.

Gesneriad culture. Propagate by cuttings, seeds.

× Gloxinera   *Gesneriaceae*

An intergeneric hybrid between *Sinningia* and *Rechsteineria,* combining the best characteristics of both parents. Gloxinia-like tubers and pink, white or yellow slipper flowers in abundance for six to eight months before a short dry rest is required. Especially recommended is × *Gloxinera* 'Bernice'—one of the most satisfactory, dependable flowering plants in my entire collection.

Culture same as for *Sinningia speciosa,* except that the resting period of the tuber may be very brief. Propagate by cuttings.

Gloxinia perennis   *Gesneriaceae*

An erect, very tall plant with metallic colored foliage which starts maroon or purplish and may change to gray, many large downy bluish flowers like Canterbury bells. This is the true *gloxinia* species and, unlike the florist's gloxinia (*Sinningia speciosa*), grows from scaly rhizomes.

Culture same as for achimenes. Propagate by cuttings, rhizomes, seeds.

Grevillea robusta   *Proteaceae*   Silk Oak

A fast growing fernlike tree that is a fine pot plant under fluorescent lights for about one year from cuttings or seed. Then it is usually too big to manage under lights.

Day neutral, 6 to 8 inches, moderate, all purpose medium, moist. Propagate from cuttings, or it is extraordinarily easy from seeds.

Gynura aurantiaca   *Compositae*   Velvet Plant

The jagged-toothed velvety leaves are densely covered with violet or purple hairs. This plant must have good light to retain its regal coloring, and fluorescent light suits it fine. It also produces its clusters of yellow or orange flowers under the lights. The plant, however, will take over the whole garden if given half a chance, and I prefer to start new plants from tip cuttings about twice a year.

Day neutral, 4 inches, warm, all purpose medium kept moist.

Haworthia   *Liliaceae*   Aristocrat Plant

Very slow growing tight pinwheels of thick, pointed leaves studded or warted with white pinheads in varied patterns. In nature shade-loving plants, haworthias flower year after year for me under fluorescent lights. The flowers are no great shakes —you just notice one day that a long threadlike stem has shot from the plant. Follow the stem to its end, which will probably be visiting an unrelated plant a foot away, and there you will find the minute white or greenish flowers.

Succulent culture. Propagate by offsets.

Hedera Helix   *Araliaceae*   English Ivy

Is there an indoor gardener who can get along without a bit of English ivy? The considerable number of *Hedera Helix* forms available are usually not hybrids but sports or mutants which, when removed from the plant on which they appeared, are capable of growing by themselves and of being reproduced vegetatively. The corner upright supports of my triple-deck fluorescent lighted benches are studded with pots of ivy hooked onto plant hangers. The pots are carried to the sink for watering and spray washing. It is difficult to keep pace with ivy nomenclature, because the mutants often mutate further and get a new name, or they may revert to their original form and drop from cultivation. Here are some *Hedera Helix* forms that I love: 'Curlilocks', *digitata,* 'Fan', 'Fluffy Ruffles', 'Glacier' (also called 'Iceberg'), 'Gold Dust', 'Goldheart', 'Itsy Bitsy', 'Ivalace', 'Jubilee', 'Manda's Crested', 'Needlepoint', *pedata* (birdsfoot ivy), 'Shamrock', 'Star', 'Sweetheart', 'Telecurl' and *walthamensis* (baby ivy).

Day neutral, 8 to 10 inches from lamps or reflected light from a large fluorescent light installation, cool to moderate, all purpose medium, moist. Mist or spray-wash the plants frequently.

Heliotropium 'Cherry Pie'   *Boraginaceae*   Heliotrope

A 12- to 15-inch high plant (small for a heliotrope), grown as an annual from seed. The white, violet, purple, or blue flowers are not spectacular, and neither is the plant, but I like to have it around for the delightful fragrance.

Day neutral, 4 to 6 inches, warm, all purpose medium, moist.

Hibiscus Rosa-sinensis var. *Cooperi*   *Malvaceae*
Rose of China, Chinese Hibiscus

One of the most ornamental of all variegated plants, and one that I love dearly. The narrow leaves are metallic green brightly variegated and marbled with dark olive, white, pink and crimson. The plant must be watered frequently or kept in a container large enough to provide plenty of root room. Otherwise the buds of its small scarlet flowers will drop. Prune the plant once or twice a year to keep it within the bounds of an indoor fluorescent light garden.

Day neutral, 6 to 8 inches, moderate, all purpose medium kept moist. Propagate by tip cuttings.

Hippeastrum   *Amaryllidaceae*   Amaryllis

The gorgeous flowers of these tender bulbs are produced on stems (when grown under lights) just about half as tall as the same plants grown on a window sill. Start the bulbs 8 to 10 inches below the lamps and keep the flower scape just clear of the tubes as it grows, which is quickly. Follow the usual amaryllis summer culture after flowering and grow the same bulbs year after year under lights.

Day neutral, moderate, all purpose medium, moist.

Hoffmannia refulgens   *Rubiaceae*   Corduroy Plant

Primarily foliage plants of dark green and dark red, somewhat iridescent, velvet above and wine-red beneath. A low, compact plant whose foliage colors are intensified by fluorescent light, although I believe they grow in shady situations in nature. Mine produced 3/4-inch pale red flowers in cymes in its second year under lights.

Day neutral, 4 to 6 inches, warm, all purpose medium, moist. Propagate by cuttings.

Hoya   *Asclepiadaceae*   Wax Plant

Indispensable is the word for hoyas. I have no *Hoya carnosa* but several plants of its variety, *H. carnosa* var. *variegata*, which has fresh to bluish green leaves bordered and splotched with creamy white and pink. Some leaves are entirely white and some entirely pink. *Variegata* climbs around the uprights of our triple-deck benches and flowers alongside fluorescent lamps fastened vertically to the uprights. It can be grown as a bushy plant if carefully pruned, but as it flowers on the previous year's stems, I prefer to let it grow as it will. The clusters of waxy fragrant starlike flowers are so perfectly formed they seem more artificial than the cheapest synthetic flower. *Hoya bella*, the miniature wax plant, has small thick green leaves on soft arching stems, and the same incredible pink and white flowers. As I write this, I can see a *Hoya bella* in a 2-inch pot, the stems trained on a small trellis in the pot, and six unbelievable flower clusters whose weight tumbled the pot over on its side until I wedged it between two pieces of shale.

Day neutral, 4 to 6 inches, warm, all purpose medium kept wet while plant is flowering, on the dry side when resting. Hoyas do not change in appearance when they rest, they merely do not produce flowers for a little while. Propagate by cuttings.

Hypocyrta   *Gesneriaceae*   Pouch Flower

The trailing and upright species are all good under fluorescent light culture. The flowers are of an unusual swollen shape. Some hypocyrtas drop their leaves and rest after flowering. In dormancy they appear hopelessly dead, but when they are good and ready they start new growth. *H. nummularia* is a compact trailer with tiny round leaves and vermilion flowers. *H. Selloana* is an upright plant with reddish flowers, seems not to take a rest. *H. strigillosa* trails, has scarlet flowers marked with yellow. *H. Wettsteinii* is a lush trailer with tiny glossy dark green leaves, red underneath, on dark red stems, abundant orange flowers for a long period.

Gesneriad culture. Propagate by cuttings.

Impatiens   *Balsaminaceae*   Patience Plant

I can have more fun with a packet of mixed dwarf impatiens seeds than I don't know what. From them grow compact pot plants that flower the year around under lights. *Impatiens repens* is a creeper with red stems, plump button shaped leaves and little yellow flowers—hard to believe it is closely related to "patient Lucy."

Day neutral, 4 to 10 inches, moderate, all purpose medium, moist. Propagate by seeds or cuttings.

Iresine Lindenii　　　*Amaranthaceae*　　　Bloodleaf

This iresine is called Achyranthes by gardeners and is used extensively as a bedding plant in parks and public gardens. I find it a delightful, colorful small pot plant that produces small white flowers continuously under fluorescent lights. The plant runs out of water quite abruptly and wilts with a dramatic shrug, yet it does not tolerate water standing around its roots. I think it possible that the plant I bought as Achyranthes is really Alternanthera, but the grower says his father called it Achyranthes and he sees no reason to change labels now.

Day neutral, 6 to 8 inches, moderate to warm, all purpose medium kept moist.

Jacobinia suberecta　　　*Acanthaceae*

A plant about 12 inches high with soft hairy leaves and orange flowers. A compact plant that sprawls, if such a thing is possible, and it should be renewed by means of tip cuttings after flowering, and the old plant discarded.

Kalanchoe　　　*Crassulaceae*

Succulent plants that are indifferent to temperature extremes and like a dry atmosphere and paucity of water. They are just plain pretty with fluorescent light culture, and I try almost any that come to my attention. *K. Blossfeldiana* 'Tom Thumb' is a dwarf plant with overlapping fresh green leaves smothered with bright red flowers. Buds are initiated during short days (6 to 8 hours of light) but a plant that has started its buds and flowers will continue to produce them for up to eight months when the plant is placed under fluorescent lights. *K. tomentosa* is the charming little panda plant—fat felty leaves with chocolate icing on the edges. *K. Diagremontiana (Bryophyllum Diagremontianum)* and *K. verticillata (Bryophyllum tubiflorum)* produce plantlets on the serrated leaf margins.

Succulent culture. Propagate by cuttings, plantlets.

Kleinia   *Compositae*

Another group of interesting succulent plants. *K. articulata,* the candle plant, can be held to 12 to 14 inches in height under fluorescent lights, and the blue leaves that grow from the ends of the candles are a curiosity. *K. repens* is low and semi-trailing with thick leaves shaped like the segments of an orange and very blue. *K. tomentosa* has cocoon-like leaves covered with white down. *K. Mandraliscae,* called blue chalk sticks, is a dusky powder blue all over.

Succulent culture.

Koellikeria erinoides   *Gesneriaceae*   Dwarf Bellflower

A sweetheart of a dwarf flowering plant. The rosettes of small green velvet leaves are sprinkled with specks of silver that actually shine. Miniature spikes of tiny two-colored bell flowers, creamy white and red, are produced abundantly. The plants grow from scaly rhizomes.

Culture same as for achimenes. Propagate by cuttings, rhizomes, seeds.

Kohleria   *Gesneriaceae*
(formerly *Tydaea* or *Isoloma)*

Upright plants that may arch or even trail, kohlerias have velvety leaves and brightly colored and variously spotted hairy flowers. They grow from scaly rhizomes. *K. amabilis* stays small and compact when given good light, produces rose colored flowers with purple dots for several months. *K. bogotensis* has red-spotted yellow flowers and rich brown leaves with a darker brown pattern. The hybrids of *K. eriantha* have velvety green leaves with a fine red border, orange-red flowers on tall plants. *K. Lindeniana* has a dwarf habit, beautifully patterned leaves and violet and white flowers. K. 'Lindy Lou' is an interspecific hybrid between *K. Lindeniana* and *K. tubiflora,* has flowers like *Lindeniana* but bigger and bolder. K. 'Longwood' is a sterile hybrid imported from Portugal, practically everblooming enormous red flowers on a tall plant.

Gesneriad culture. Propagate by cuttings, rhizomes, seeds.

Lantana   *Verbenaceae*

Given sufficient light, lantanas are honestly everblooming plants, although they become straggly and need a good pruning about twice a year. *L. montevidensis,* the weeping or trailing lavender lantana, is good in pots at the edge of a bench, where it can trail down. Dwarf forms of the garden lantana, *L. Camara,* are excellent and delightful in pots, being prolific bloomers of verbena-like flowers that open pink or yellow and darken to red or orange; usually several different shades are on the same plant at the same time. I have banned lantanas from my fluorescent light gardens, however, because I seem to find white flies every time I put a lantana plant in the indoor garden. I do not care much for insects so will do my lantana growing outdoors in the summer time.

Day neutral, 6 to 8 inches, moderate, all purpose medium kept on the dry side except that the root ball should not dry out. Propagate by cuttings, seeds.

Lobelia   *Lobeliaceae*

I recommend 'Hamburgia', 'Sapphire' and 'Blue Cascade'. Grown from seed, they are absolutely delightful dainty trailing cascades of azure blue and Cambridge blue flowers when placed at the bench edge and allowed to trail down. They are not supposed to be indoor plants, but I was hungry for truly blue flowers among the riotous reds and pinks and oranges of the tropical plants, and tried the lobelias.

Day neutral, 8 to 10 inches, moderate, all purpose medium, moist. Propagate by seeds.

Lysionotus serratus   *Gesneriaceae*   Oriental Bellflower

A small shrub 8 to 10 inches in height with clusters of pale lilac tubular flowers.

Gesneriad culture. Propagate by seeds or cuttings.

Malpighia coccigera   *Malpighiaceae*   Miniature Holly

A diminutive evergreen plant with small glossy leaves sharply toothed like holly, small fluffy pale pink flowers.

Day neutral, 8 to 10 inches, warm, all purpose medium, moist. Propagate by stem cuttings.

Manettia bicolor   *Rubiaceae*   Mexican Firecracker

Impudent, ½-inch long yellow-tipped red flowers pop out all over twining threadlike stems of this plant. It will climb on anything it touches, but I prune it severely and grow it as a bushy pot plant.

Day neutral, 6 to 8 inches, moderate, all purpose medium, moist. Propagate by cuttings or seeds.

Maranta   *Marantaceae*

Marantas differ from calatheas only in technical, not in obvious, characteristics. They are exotic plants whose foliage reminds me of iridescent taffeta. Young plants are prettiest, the beautiful markings may disappear as a plant ages. *M. leuconeura* var. *Kerchoveana,* rabbit tracks or prayer plant, folds its leaves at night to funnel the moisture to the roots. *L. leuconeura* var. *Massangeana* is similar but has smaller leaves purple underneath.

Day neutral, 8 to 10 inches, warm, 60% or more humidity, all purpose medium, moist except when plant is resting—then it should be allowed to dry out between waterings. Propagate by dividing the crown.

Melaleuca hypericifolia   *Myrtaceae*   Bottle Brush

Similar to *Callistemon viminalis* in flowers and culture, with the grand exception that the leaves smell like Mentholatum when crushed.

Mimosa pudica   *Leguminosae*   Sensitive Plant
                                                  Humble Plant

This foolish little plant runs wild in our Gulf states but must be grown as a pot plant indoors in the North. It has feathery leaves that fold in humility when they are touched. I have never seen its heads of lavender flowers. I grow two or three plants from seed every year, just for their conversation value and to intrigue juvenile guests.

Day neutral, 6 to 8 inches, moderate to warm, all purpose medium, moist. Propagate annually from seeds.

Myrsine africana   *Myrsinaceae*   African Boxwood

A shrubby little bush resembling boxwood, but more graceful. Small, shiny dark green ½-inch long leaves. Fun to grow and shape into miniature patterns like true boxwood.

Day neutral, 8 to 10 inches, moderate, all purpose medium, moist. Propagate by stem cuttings.

Myrtus communis var. microphylla   *Myrtaceae*
                                                  Dwarf Greek Myrtle

Resembles English box and may be sheared to any shape you like. The foliage, not the flower, is aromatic, so it does not matter that constant pruning prevents flowering.

Day neutral, 8 to 10 inches, moderate, all purpose medium, moist. Propagate by stem cuttings.

Nautilocalyx   *Gesneriaceae*

Erect, shrubby plants with attractive leaves and inconspicuous but interesting pale yellow flowers. *N. bullatus* is a dark brown bubbly-leaved species, once incorrectly called *Episcia tesselata*. *N. Forgetii* has bright green leaves with a darker pattern, wavy edges, and yellow flowers covered with fine hairs. *N. Lynchii* leaves are so dark a maroon as to appear almost black, red midrib, reddish purple underneath.

Gesneriad culture. Propagate by tip cuttings.

Nematanthus longipes   *Gesneriaceae*

A Peruvian trailing plant with thick smooth green leaves and two-inch long flaming red flowers that dangle from very long pedicels.

Gesneriad culture. Propagate by cuttings.

Nicotiana   *Solanaceae*   Flowering Tobacco

Many forms of nicotiana close their flowers in bright light and open them and release their fragrance at night. Some dwarf hybrids keep their flowers open in bright light and grow and flower well as pot plants in a fluorescent light garden. Two such are 'White Bedder' and 'Crimson Bedder'.

Day neutral, 4 to 6 inches, moderate, all purpose medium, moist. Propagate by seeds, cuttings.

Orchid   *Orchidaceae*   Orchid

The culture of orchids under fluorescent light differs considerably from growth in a greenhouse or on a window sill. It is

FIG. 36   A fluorescent light orchid garden.

[Mr. and Mrs. Thomas Powell]

both more challenging and more rewarding. Under lights, many
orchids produce more mature growths in a year than they would
in a greenhouse, with more and bigger flowers, and they continue in healthy active growth without requiring a rest period.
Successful growers say that virtually any orchid will grow and
flower well under fluorescent lights, provided of course that its
other requirements such as temperature and humidity are met
to a reasonable degree.

   Mr. and Mrs. Thomas Powell, of New York City, grow many

kinds of orchids under fluorescent light. They advise that cattleyas, cymbidiums, dendrobiums, epidendrums, oncidiums and vandas need a minimum of 1,000 footcandles and should be placed under the centers of the tubes. Cypripediums, phalaenopsis, and other shade-loving orchids require a minimum of 700 footcandles and do well when placed under the ends of the tubes or on the fringes of the lighted area. The plants can almost touch the lamps, as the fluorescent tubes will not burn the foliage.

Little is known about the photoperiodic response of orchids, that is, how seasonal changes in length of day and night affect their blooming. Most growers of orchids indoors give their plants 14 hours of fluorescent light per day throughout the year, using a one-to-one combination of cool white and warm white tubes, or daylight and natural tubes, or daylight and deluxe warm white tubes. Gro-Lux tubes also appear to be highly useful. However, as Gro-Lux lamps produce about twice the total effective light energy of other tubes, most growers give their orchids somewhat more fertilizer when growing under Gro-Lux, in order to keep the sun-food ratio in balance.

For purposes of culture, orchids fall into three groups: the cool, which require a 45- to 50-degree night temperature; the intermediate, which do best at a minimum night temperature of 55 to 60 degrees; and the warm, which need 60 to 65 degrees at night. The great majority of orchids fall into the intermediate group.

Orchids like a relative humidity of 50 to 60 per cent. The easiest way to provide humidity for orchids is to place the plants on trays of gravel, with the water level in the trays kept just below the top of the gravel. The roots will rot if the pot contacts the water. The plants should also be mist-sprayed daily in hot weather. Good air circulation is very important to orchids, as they do not like a stuffy atmosphere.

Watering should be done only when the potting medium becomes nearly bone dry. For many mature plants, this may mean watering only once or twice a week, but seedlings or miniature orchids in tiny pots will need watering more frequently. While each grower must work out a schedule to suit his own conditions, a good rule is to err on the dry side rather than the wet—overwatering is the biggest single reason for failure with orchids. Exceptions to this rule are cypripediums and phalaenopsis, which prefer a constantly moist (but not soaking wet) medium.

Orchids planted in osmunda (fern root) need no fertilization, but those in fir bark or bark mixes should be given a 20-20-20 or similar formula every ten days to two weeks. Some growers supplement this mineral fertilizer with fish emulsion twice a month to provide trace elements. Repotting, and dividing if necessary, is generally done every two years, after flowering.

Of the many orchids that do well under lights, the miniatures—small in size of plant but not necessarily in size of flower—are especially interesting. *Brassavola nodosa,* the charming "lady of the night," which flowers normally in the fall, has flowered twice in one year and is preparing to flower for the third time in fourteen months in my fluorescent light garden. I love it for the spicy fragrance it pours forth after the lights are turned off at night. Other miniatures that bloom well under lights are *Oncidium cheirophorum,* which smells like beer; the little "mealy bug" orchid, *Ornithocephalus bicornis; Dendrobium Jenkinsii,* with pretty yellow flowers; the white and lavender *Laelia lundii regnellii;* the "coral" orchid, *Rodriguezia secunda;* and many others of myriad colors and forms. In larger plants, I have found the lovely green and white "lady slipper," *Cypripedium Maudiae,* especially rewarding—it has flowered twice in ten months under my lights.

Experienced growers recommend the above plants, as well as

both species and hybrid cattleyas, epidendrum, laelia, and oncidiums as excellent plants for the beginner, as they adapt easily to growing under fluorescent light. Orchids, incidentally, are among the most adaptable of plants, and it is not unusual to see cool varieties growing and flowering well in the same growing area as intermediate or even warm types. The majority of orchids appear able to accommodate themselves to widely varying environments and cultural practices.

Mr. and Mrs. Powell say they have seen orchids thriving under all sorts of fluorescent light setups, including plant carts and Wardian cases, as well as homemade arrangements built into hi-fi cabinets, room dividers and even delicatessen cases!

One final point: fluorescent lights are particularly valuable for orchid seedlings. Cattleyas, for example, generally take from five to seven years from seed sowing to first flowering. Under lights, however, with up to 4,000 footcandles for 16 hours a day and high levels of water and nutrients, orchids have been raised from seed to flower in less than three years.

Osmanthus fragrans   *Oleaceae*   Flowering Olive

A 30-foot tree in its native Asia but a highly satisfactory plant in a 4- to 6-inch pot under lights. An evergreen plant with dark green shiny foliage that bears deliciously sweet white flowers during most of the year, when kept potbound.

Day neutral, 4 to 6 inches, moderate, all purpose medium, moist, tolerates a dry atmosphere remarkably well. Propagate by cuttings.

Oxalis hedysaroides rubra   *Oxalidaceae*   Firefern

A beautiful slow-growing plant amenable to pinching. Erect, shrubby, with many wiry stems and delicate fernlike foliage of glowing, satiny wine red, many little bright yellow flowers. Fluorescent light enhances the thin silky foliage. The plant is particularly sensitive to any change in its culture—a draft, too much fertilizer, a move from one location to another, can cause it to drop all its beautiful leaves. It adjusts quickly, however, and regrows what it has lost. One of my plants went through this skeletonizing procedure at least a dozen times, until I learned not to move it around.

Day neutral, 4 to 6 inches, warm, all purpose medium slightly on the dry side. Propagate by cuttings.

Pelargonium   *Geraniaceae*   Geranium

All geraniums—miniature, dwarf, semidwarf, fancy-leaved, scented-leaved, ivy-leaved, garden varieties, and collectors' choice—need strong light. "Strong light" means 850 to 1,200 footcandles, or a distance of 1 to 3 inches between top of plant and fluorescent tube, 14 to 18 hours a day. As the plants grow, the tops should be pinched out to make the plants grow full and bushy.

It is impractical to grow and flower the large zonal geraniums and the big species pelargoniums under fluorescent lights, but only because of their size and the space they require. If you love these plants, and can afford the space and electricity, do set up a fluorescent light garden for them.

Generally, the ideal geranium growing conditions, in addition to the strong light mentioned, include a daytime temperature of 65 to 70 degrees, a night temperature of 55 to 60 degrees, a relative humidity of 40 to 50 per cent, a friable growing medium that drains quickly and well and is just slightly acid (pH 6.5), and watering when the surface of the soil feels dry to the touch.

The miniature, dwarf, and semidwarf geraniums are sweet

gems in a fluorescent light garden. Their diminutive stature and small space requirements endear them to an indoor gardener, but these features also allow the wee plants to be overlooked or lost when placed among bigger, more vigorous plants. I boost a wire platform by means of an inverted flower pot at each corner, and place the small geraniums on the platform, with the tops of the plants within 3 inches of the lamps. The miniatures grow slowly, and they do require about a 50 per cent relative humidity to keep foliage and flower buds from browning and blasting. The geranium specialists have outdone themselves in creating new cultivars of these tiny plants for our enjoyment, and the plants are named so enchantingly. The first time I saw a list of miniature geraniums, I thought I might be happy just to grow the labels! Try these miniature and dwarf geraniums: 'Milky Way' and 'Small Fortune' with white flowers; 'Gypsy Gem' and 'Tweedle Dum', salmon flowers; 'Black Vesuvius', 'Mischief', orange flowers; 'Imp', 'Pixie', salmon pink flowers; 'Tiny Tim', 'Kleiner Liebling', pink, rose flowers; 'Dee Dee', scarlet flowers; 'Firefly', 'Goblin', 'Perky', 'Tiny Tim', red flowers. And these semidwarf geraniums: 'Snow White', 'Dopey', 'Doc', and 'Sneezy'.

Fancy-leaved geraniums belong in a fluorescent light garden, too. The constant supply of fluorescent light develops colors in the foliage that one does not see in plants grown on a window sill or in a greenhouse. Try 'Mrs. Cox', 'Skies of Italy', 'Filigree', 'Alpha', 'Black Jubilee', two butterfly geraniums, 'Happy Thought' and 'Crystal Palace Gem', and some of the fancy-leaved dwarf geraniums as 'Little Trot' and 'Sprite'.

There are eight groups of scented-leaved geraniums from which to select the scent you like best. I have two favorites: *Pelargonium tomentosum* (peppermint scented) and *P. crispum,* the finger-bowl lemon-scented geranium with very small leaves.

The hybrids of *Pelargonium* × *domesticum*—variously called Lady Washington, Martha Washington, Regal, Fancy, Show, and Royal—are different in appearance and culture from the other geraniums. They definitely require winter rest in a 40- to 50-degree temperature. I agree with the devotees of Lady Washington geraniums that the flowers are among the most beautiful of all cultivated plants, but for some reason I have never warmed up to these plants and have not tried to grow them with fluorescent light. The few pots I have of them are wintered over under a bench in the cool greenhouse.

Fluorescent lights are useful in other phases of geranium culture: to grow seedlings to maturity; to root cuttings; to carry large geraniums safely through the winter; and to winter tree geraniums. Just take care never to crowd geraniums close together.

Do send for the catalogs of the geranium specialists who are listed in this book. Maybe you will be as undecided as to what sort of geranium to buy next as I am!

Pellionia   *Urticaceae*

Delicate tropical creepers that I like to plant on the floor of a terrarium under lights. *P. pulchra* has dusty blue-gray leaves with black lines, violet underneath, and lavender-pink stems. *P. repens (Daveauana)* leaves are oval, metallic copper-green with chartreuse on both sides of the center nerve.

Day neutral, 10 to 12 inches, warm and humid, all purpose medium or moss, moist. Propagate by cuttings, divisions of rooted stems.

Peperomia   *Piperaceae*

I think I am safe in saying that any peperomia that comes your way will grow beautifully in your fluorescent light garden.

They flower more often with fluorescent light culture than they do on a window sill but the miniature cattail-like flowers are something one just puts up with. I have twenty-some species and hybrids in baskets and pots. They are as dependable as the electric light bill.

Succulent culture—overwatering is the one sure way to kill a peperomia. Propogate by cuttings, divisions.

Pilea   Urticaceae

With one exception a genus of creeping plants. I grow the creepers in terrariums under lights. *P. cadierei* is the upright popular aluminum plant; its dwarf form is *P. cadieri minima*. *P. nummulariaefolia* is called creeping Charlie. *P. microphylla* is the artillery plant. P. 'Silver Tree' is a trade name for a species with brown-green leaves with a broad silver zone on each side of the center vein.

Day neutral, 10 to 12 inches, warm and humid, all purpose medium or moss, moist. Propagate by cuttings on bottom heat.

Pleispilos   Aizoceae   Living Rocks

Small stemless succulents with pairs of thick, stone-like leaves about two inches long and broad, flattened inside, light gray-green with numerous dark green dots. Flowers deep yellow. These plants usually have only one pair of live leaves. A pair of shrivelled leaves under the live ones is a natural condition. The dead leaves should not be removed until they fall away of their own accord, as they nourish the new leaves. *P. bolusii* and *P. Nelii* are two that I like.

Succulent culture.

Punica Granatum var. nana   *Punicaceae*

Pomegranate

A long-lived little tree, evergreen when grown in light and warmth, deciduous if grown on a cool porch. Flowers on and off during the year under lights, and occasionally the orange flowers are followed by disproportionately large fruits.

Day neutral, 8 to 10 inches, moderate, heavy loam, moist. Propagate by cuttings, seeds.

Rechsteineria   *Gesneriaceae*

Many clusters of brilliant red helmet-shaped flowers, the softest imaginable downy leaves. Grows from a woody tuber which pushes above the soil. Tuber increases in size and produces a larger plant each year. The plants are naturally upright but may become viney in poor light. Most rechsteinerias take very little, sometimes no, dormant period. *R. cardinalis*, long tubular scarlet blooms and bright green soft velvety leaves. *R. leucotricha*, small salmon-colored flowers, leaves and stems like soft gray-green velour—this rechsteineria takes a six-month rest after flowering. *R. cyclophylla*, neon red flowers soon after potting.

Culture same as *Sinningia speciosa*. Propagate by cuttings, tubers, seeds.

Rosa   *Rosaceae*   Rose

Roses are not by nature indoor plants, and, though I may be drummed out of the corps for admitting it, I am not very fond of roses. So I have grown less than twenty under lights— just enough to know that it can be done. The half-dozen or so hybrid tea roses that grace our patio during the summer are planted in large wooden buckets. The plants are usually still budding and flowering when the days begin to shorten and the weather cools. We move the buckets of roses to the cool greenhouse where the plants continue to flower under the fluorescent lights until January. Then, still in the containers, the plants are laid on their sides in a coldframe, covered with salt hay, and brought out for the next summer's performance at the appropriate time in the spring. The same plants in the same buckets have gone through this routine for six years now, and our guests who adore roses say the flowers are prettier every year. Yes, the plants get the prescribed attentions to fertilizing and spraying.

The above information is probably not at all exciting to an indoor gardener who has no summer roses in a yard, no greenhouse, and no coldframe. Having observed flower show visitors pressing around the counters of miniature roses at spring shows, I assume that a lot of people love these little plants and, judging by the clang of the cash register, many people buy them for window sill or indoor growing. So I have tried them under fluorescent lights, and I must say, they are all right.

Buy your miniature rose plants in the fall or early winter, at a local garden center or from a miniature-rose specialist. Insist on pot-grown plants—the root disturbance that occurs when a ground-grown plant is dug and sent to you to plant in a pot is likely to set the plant back several months. Mail-order plants usually arrive with the soil ball intact about the roots, the stems cut back to 2 to 3 inches.

Miniature roses are naturally deep-rooted plants, so they require a standard pot, that is, one with the greatest depth. I have found no difference between clay and plastic pots in successful miniature rose growing. Generally the small new plants can be started in 3-inch pots and shifted to 4-inch pots before the plants become acutely rootbound. The larger miniatures—those that reach 10 to 12 inches in height—may need larger

pots. Pack a fairly heavy potting soil quite firmly in the pot. I
use my all purpose mix with an extra ration of sand, and I have
used a prepared African violet mix with a little extra sand
added to it.

Light, temperature, and humidity are the three vital cultural
requirements for miniature roses indoors. My plants are grown
4 to 6 inches below Gro-Lux lamps, lights burning for 14 hours
a day. The experts advise that the plants should never have a
temperature of more than 70° and that 65° or even much
lower is preferred. I wanted my miniature roses indoors in the
plant room where the daytime temperature sometimes goes
close to 80° during the winter, and took the chance of trying to
grow them there. The plants in the higher temperatures per-
formed just as well as those I grew under lights in the cool
greenhouse, but probably only because I was able to provide the
third cultural requirement, humidity. I misted the foliage at
least once a day, and covered the plants with plastic tents every
night. The soil should be always just moist. The plants should
be fertilized with a rose food according to package directions
and at half the recommended strength, or every three weeks
with a soluble house-plant fertilizer (not one high in nitrogen)
in half-strength solution. Several of the miniature rose plants
displayed symptoms of iron deficiency, which was corrected
quickly by applying $\frac{1}{8}$ teaspoon of Sequestrene iron chelate to
the surface of the soil and washing it into the soil with water.

The only pruning and grooming required is to remove faded
flowers promptly and snip off the occasional stem that shoots
out unattractively. The plants do like a weekly foliage washing
at the sink. A weekly preventive spraying with a house-plant
aerosol bomb takes care of insects and disease.

After my miniature roses had flowered all winter and spring,
I set the pots in a shady corner of the terrace for the summer,
cut them back to 2 inches in October, and brought them into

the fluorescent light garden where they repeated the first year's performance. At the end of the second year I moved the plants to a permanent home in the ground outdoors, so I do not know how many years they could be grown indoors without having the cold winter rest that a rose's nature requires.

These are some miniatures that grew and flowered for me under lights: 'Baby Crimson', 'Bo-Peep', 'Cinderella', 'Little Princess', 'Perle d'Alcanada', 'Pixie Gold', 'Red Imp', 'Rosata', 'Scarlet Gem', 'Sunbeam', 'Thumbelina', 'Yellow Miniature'.

Contrary to the flamboyant advertisements, miniature rose plants do not flower continuously. They flower for a few weeks, then rest a bit before budding and flowering again. This is true whether the plants are outdoors, in a cool greenhouse, or under fluorescent lights.

Writing this has made me realize that I really *did* like those little roses. I think I will order a miniature climbing rose and a miniature tree rose for the coming winter, and see how they will grow in the fluorescent light garden.

Saintpaulia   *Gesneriaceae*   African Violet

African violets grow to perfection under fluorescent light, if their other requirements are met. The balance of temperature, relative humidity, fertilizing, amount of light and distance from lamps seems to be rather critical, and the grower just starting to grow African violets under lights may have to adjust one or more of these factors until he strikes the right combination. Experience shows that African violets do not require as intense a light as, for example, gloxinias, and yet one can just miss giving them enough (by having them too far away from the lamps), causing them to grow upward instead of outward in the beautiful rosette form that is so universally admired. Generally, African violets need 14 hours of light a day, and additional hours up to 16 do not seem to help or harm them. The consensus among my friends who grow bench upon bench of African violets under fluorescent lights is that the light period should be reduced to 10 to 12 hours a day during periods of extreme heat, but that the regular fertilizing program should be maintained during that time.

African violet varieties with dark green foliage should be 10 to 12 inches below the *center* of white fluorescent lamps, 12 to 14 inches below the *center* of Gro-Lux lamps. Varieties with light green or variegated foliage, and those with "strawberry" type foliage, need less light and should be the distances mentioned below the *ends* of the fluorescent lamps, or at the outer edges of the growing area. Some of the varieties that produce white or light pink flowers also do better under the *ends* of the lamps. It would almost seem that if the lights were placed a greater distance away from African violets with light green or variegated foliage, the plants should grow satisfactorily under the center of the tube, but this results in tall-growing, sprawly plants, and it is better to give them the lesser amount of light they need by placing them under the ends of the lamps or at the outer edges of the bench.

Too much light on an African violet can cause the plant to bunch and tighten in the center and turn gray—the symptom is much like that of an infestation of cyclamen mite. Too much light can cause variegated African violet foliage to revert to solid green; technically, this amounts to making a sick plant well again because the variegation in plant foliage is actually an abnormal distribution or absence of chlorophyll.

Saxifraga sarmentosa   *Saxifragaceae*   Strawberry
Begonia, Strawberry Geranium

A hardy perennial that grows equally well indoors. Round
silver-veined leaves grow in rosette fashion from the crown,
which also sends out thin red stems in the manner of a strawberry plant, with new little plants that root and grow wherever
they touch soil. The miniature tricolor variety 'Magic Carpet',
has a touch of red and pink in the foliage.

Day neutral, 6 to 8 inches, cool, poor soil kept dry. Propagate by runners.

Scilla hispanica   *Lilaceae*   Spanish Bluebell

An evergreen clustering bulbous plant that grows 20 inches
high in nature, but has stayed under 8 inches in four years of
growing in my fluorescent light garden, in a 2½-inch pot. Small
gray-green straplike leaves mottled with darker green, loose
racemes of small blue bell-shaped flowers once a year.

Day neutral, 10 inches, cool, all purpose medium, moist.
Propagate by offsets.

Sedum   *Crassulaceae*   Stonecrop

Tender relatives of the hardy garden sedums, requiring little
care but providing interest in their little fleshy leaves and
showy flowers. Better in baskets. *S. lineare* var. *variegatum*
has many branching stems thickly covered with creamy white
needle-shaped leaves. *S. Morganianum,* burro tail, a wonderful
blue-gray trailer with pink flowers. *S. multiceps,* the little
Joshua tree, does not go over 4 inches in height in nature, and
half that in a pot, looks like a dollhouse version of a conifer.

S. pachyphyllum, jelly beans, has fat berry-like leaves close to the branching stems, yellow flowers. *S. Stahlii,* coral beads or Boston beans, beady reddish leaves close together on branching stems, yellow flowers.

   Succulent culture.

Serissa foetida (japonica) var. *variegata*   *Rubiaceae*

A dwarf shrub with small dark green leaves margined with yellow, funnelform little white flowers.

   Day neutral, 8 to 10 inches, moderate, all purpose mix moderately moist. Propagate by cuttings.

Setcreasea purpurea 'Purple Heart'   *Commelinaceae*

A Wandering Jew, easy to grow. Pinch back frequently for bushy compact plants. This variety has large three-petaled lavender flowers, striking purple leaves covered with pale hair.

   Day neutral, 6 to 8 inches, moderate, all purpose medium, moist. Propagate by cuttings.

Sinningia species   *Gesneriaceae*

Tuberous-rooted gesneriads that have become very popular house plants, they are among the very best for fluorescent light culture. *S. eumorpha* has shiny leaves, white flowers with yellow throat striped with purple. *S. pusilla* is the tiniest tuberous gesneriad—a 1-inch pot is usually too big for it. *S.* × *pumila* 'Tetra', a cross between *pusilla* and *eumorpha,* is larger than *pusilla* but still a miniature. *S. regina* has silver veins on soft dark green leaves that are red underneath, deep purple nodding slipper flowers, a highly decorative plant. *S. tubiflora* has long white flowers, is a tall plant and requires high light levels to flower; so far as I know, it is the only distinctly fragrant gesneriad.

Culture same as for *Sinningia speciosa,* the florist's gloxinia.

Sinningia speciosa　　　　*Gesneriaceae*　　　　Gloxinia

The tuberous-rooted gloxinias we know and grow today are hybrids. (The only true gloxinia commonly grown by amateurs is *Gloxinia perennis,* which is propagated by scaly rhizomes.) The sinningia species cross readily with each other to produce plants with flowers of brilliant blues, reds, purples, pale and bright pinks, pristine whites, color dusted in speckles, color in bands and ruffles; flowers in nodding slipper shape or upright, open-faced bell shape; flowers 4 to 5 inches in diameter, with from five to nine petals. These hybrids themselves frequently cross easily with other hybrid gloxinias.

Florists grow gloxinias from seed to bloom in five to six months. This time can be shortened to 3 to 3½ months with fluorescent light culture. There is a danger in it, though: a tiny pinch of the dust-fine seeds will produce so many plants that the strongest restraint must be exercised, unless your family really likes gloxinias in the salad and gloxinias in the stew. Use moist milled sphagnum moss as a seed bed. Sow the seeds thinly on top of the moss and mist lightly with warm water to anchor them. Place the containers where they will get bottom heat, humidity and light. The container should be about 11 inches below the center or 6 to 8 inches below the ends of a lamp. The age and quality of the seed have much to do with the rate of germination. Fresh seed (ten days to two weeks old) can be expected to germinate within ten days of sowing. Older seed may take 25 to 30 days to germinate, and considerable leeway should be allowed before deciding that they just are not going to germinate. It has happened more than once that an indoor gardener has banished a container of seeds to the compost pile, only to find tiny plants growing there a few weeks later. Follow the procedure for handling tiny seedlings recommended in Chapter 7.

For a specimen gloxinia plant with abundant flowers, put the seedling directly into a 5- or 6-inch pot, where it will flower in six to eight months. For earlier but less abundant flowering—in about three months—plant the seedling in a 3- or 3½-inch pot. Expect a few laggards from a batch of seed; sometimes these are the best and well worth waiting for. Place the pots 4 to 6 inches below the lamps. As buds lift and flowers open, raise the light enough to clear the flowers.

To restart a gloxinia tuber into growth, plant one tuber to a 5- or 6-inch pot, the concave (indented) side of the tuber up. Cover the tuber with about ¾ inch of the potting medium. Gentle bottom heat is desirable for starting growth, but not essential, and the pots can be placed directly on the fluorescent-lighted bench on which they are to grow. The distance from the light is not critical at this stage. The pots can be squeezed in wherever they will fit and at any distance from the light, even in among plants whose foliage might partially shade the newly-started tuber. As soon as growth appears above the surface of the soil, the pots should be brought much closer to the light, about 3 inches from lamp to top of plant. Growth will now be rapid. All shoots except the main one should be rubbed off as they appear, or these secondary growths can be allowed to grow to about 2 inches and then be pulled off and placed in a propagating case to root. In any event, a gloxinia should be grown with a single crown. It is much more handsome than one with multiple crowns pushing each other around and requiring staking. Flower production is usually superior in quantity and quality on a single crown plant. Keep the plants close to the lamps for about ten days, then increase the distance to about 6 inches, and continue to raise the lights as the plants grow.

Smithiantha   *Gesneriaceae*   Temple Bells

Upright plants with velvety green foliage which often has decorative patterns of red, purple or brown, and exquisite bell-shaped flowers. Smithianthas are fibrous-rooted from scaly rhizomes. *S. cinnabarina* has leaves like red plush and brilliant orange flowers—if you ever see a prettier plant than this one in your fluorescent light garden I hope you will tell me what it is. The Cornell Series Smithianthas are ten hybrids created at Cornell University, choice plants, now available from gesneriad specialists. The specialists also have dwarf hybrid smithianthas, as yet unnamed, which are excellent in 3-inch pots. *S. multiflora* has dark green leaves on tall stems, white flowers with yellow throat spotted red. *S. zebrina* has velvety dark green leaves variegated brown or purple, red and yellow flowers.

Gesneriad culture, except that the plants can take all possible light and the foliage can graze the lamps. Propagate by cuttings, rhizomes, seeds.

Streptocarpus   *Gesneriaceae*   Cape Primrose

A fibrous-rooted evergreen gesneriad usually with straplike leaves, best treated as an annual though hybrids may be grown on by plant divisions. Flowers are blue, pink, white, or purple, and gloxinia-like shape. The Rexii hybrids (called cape primrose) are the big, pretty ones. A subgenus, *Streptocarpella*, contains species of branching habit—*S. Holstii* and *S. caulescens* have shiny oval leaves and many small violet-blue flowers; both are in flower in my fluorescent light garden the year around.

Another *Streptocarpella* species, *S. saxorum,* has trailing stems and white and pale lavender flowers on long wiry stems; it flowers in my greenhouse but I have not flowered it under lights and suspect that it requires a different period of darkness than most gesneriads.

Gesneriad culture. Prefers a night temperature of 50 to 55 degrees. I move streptocarpus plants to a cool corner on the floor at night. Propagate by division of plant, cuttings, seeds. Flowers first year from any of these.

Streptogloxinia   *Gesneriaceae*

So far as I know, plants sold under this name and under the name "Stroxinia" are not crosses between streptocarpus and gloxinias, as some dealers claim, but are just slipper gloxinias. Don't let the confusion about parentage deter you from growing the plants so long as you treat them as gloxinias *(Sinningia speciosa).*

Streptosolen Jamesonii   *Solanaceae*   Orange Browallia

A relative of the browallia, handled in the same manner except streptosolen prefers a night temperature of 55°.

Succulents—see Cactus

Thea sinensis   *Theaceae*   Tea

The tea of commerce is made from the leaves of *Thea sinensis.* My one plant, grown from a seed that took thirteen months to germinate, may never flower under lights in the cool greenhouse, even given the required camellia culture. Just getting it to grow has been enough.

Tibouchina semidecandra   *Melastomaceae*
                                    Glory Bush, Empress Flower

One of the very few plants whose leaf veins run vertically, this leggy plant needs constant pruning and pinching back. The velvety pale green leaves are attractive and so are the purple clematis-shaped flowers, though the latter are short-lived.

Day neutral, 6 to 8 inches, cool, all purpose medium, moist. Propagate by cuttings or seeds.

Titanotrichum Oldhamii   *Gesneriaceae*   Formo-
                                                        san Bellflower

A tall-growing (1½ to 2 feet under lights) gesneriad that grows from scaly rhizomes and produces whiplike branches of propagules after flowering, has long flower-bearing stems hung with deep chrome yellow flowers with deep red faces.

Gesneriad culture, keep moist. Propagate by rhizomes, propagules or leaf cuttings.

Tolmiea Menziesii   *Saxifragaceae*   Piggy-back
                                                    Plant

There is no particular advantage to growing this tolerant plant under lights except the novelty of seeing the tiny new leaves growing from the old leaves.

Tradescantia   *Commelinaceae*   Inch Plant
                                                  Wandering Jew

Inch plants will rambunctiously overrun an indoor garden unless kept in check, and I cannt keep up with most of them. Fluorescent light, however, enhances foliage colorings and I have a few plants. *T. multiflora* has threadlike stems, small slim plain dark green thin leaves purple underneath, and clusters of tiny white winking flowers; I let the stems grow out of and wrap around a wire basket for a delicate, ferny effect. *T. navicularis*, China plant, is a succulent creeper with very thick stems, short coppery green boat-shaped leaves, rosy-purple flowers. I also have an unidentified tradescantia with variegated green and white foliage and white flowers, which a florist assured me was the very latest in "wandering juice" plants.

Day neutral, 10 to 12 inches, moderate, all purpose medium, kept on the dry side. Propagate by cuttings, seeds, division.

ANNUALS FOR WINTER FLOWERING

The annual flowering plants that you love in your outdoor garden all summer will flower during the winter indoors under fluorescent lights. The mature size of the plant versus the available space is probably the determining factor in deciding which annuals are to be grown indoors. Given 16 to 18 hours of light a day, most of the annuals start flowering eight to twelve weeks after the date of sowing the seeds, and a late August or early September sowing will give flowering plants by late October or during November. Seeds of annuals are not always available in late summer, and I usually hold out a few seeds from my early spring sowings. The plants may not branch so well as they do outdoors, but they will bloom normally if their other cultural requirements are met.

After several years of trying to grow every available kind of ornamental plant under lights, I have concluded that I will leave the marigolds, petunias, zinnias and other annual flowering plants to their summer season out of doors, and use the space in my fluorescent light gardens for the tropical and rare plants that I cannot raise outside.

VEGETABLES AND FLOWERING ANNUALS FOR THE OUTDOOR GARDEN

A very small amount of money spent for seeds will buy a beautiful summer garden, and a healthful one, too. There is probably no more practical application of fluorescent light to gardening than its use in growing the seedlings and plants of garden vegetables and annual and perennial flowers for the outdoor garden. Many a dirt gardener who would not dream of burning electric lights all winter for an indoor flower garden uses fluorescent light as a matter of course to start his outdoor garden and be way ahead of the neighbors in flowers and truck garden produce.

Like most of you to whom a seed catalog is more fascinating than a best-selling novel, I order seeds early so they are received in January. The procedure to be followed depends on the habits of the plant and the date on which you can expect to put the plants outdoors. In my area, May 15 is considered to be the average date on which the last frost can be expected. I count back from that date the number of weeks which the seed packet recommends as being required to have plants ready for transplanting to the ground.

My seeds are planted in individual plastic containers of

milled sphagnum moss which are placed in an electric propagating case where they have bottom heat and humidity. The
propagating cases are placed directly under Gro-Lux lamps.
The containers of the seeds that must be germinated in darkness (the seed packet usually gives this information) are covered
with something opaque until the seeds germinate. The "something opaque" in my case are pieces of vinyl tile left from a
floor covering project.

Seedlings are handled as described in Chapter 7, being transplanted to small flats within a few days of germination. When
the leaves touch, the plants are moved to individual peat pots.
I prefer the square peat pots because they line up easily in a
wooden flat with no waste space between pots.

Vegetable and bedding plant seedlings can use as much light
as you can possibly give them, for 18 and not less than 14
hours a day. Keep the tops of the plants within 3 inches of
the tubes. The plants grow quickly and daily attention is required to keep the lamps 2 to 3 inches above the plants. It is
better not to let tender seedlings actually touch the tubes. The
foliage probably will not literally burn, but the plants grow
so quickly that within 24 hours they can achieve a permanent
distortion in shape or form in their efforts to grow around a
tube. Each seedling must have enough room to grow its side
branches. Crowded plants grow straight up with one spindly
stalk which will flower but the plant will never amount to
anything.

The seedlings grow best in a temperature range of 55 to 60
degrees at night. Daytime temperature may be ten degrees
higher, but when the lights are off the lower temperature is
required. A constant temperature of 70 to 80 degrees produces
spindly plants, and the whole purpose of starting the plants
under fluorescent lights is defeated. Seeds requiring 65 to 75

degrees to germinate should be grown on in the 55- to 60-degree temperature range.

Vegetable and annual seedlings must not dry out. Drying stunts growth and often kills the plants. Fertilize the fast-growing types of seedlings twice a week, the slower ones once a week.

The seedlings must have a gradual adjustment to their out-of-door situation. We improvised a shading arrangement of a length of wide-mesh pliable wire fencing through which we wove aluminum slats from a discarded Venetian blind. We place the wooden flats of peat pots on the unroofed terrace with the shading device bent over them in the shape of a Quonset hut. It would be too much of a chore to carry all the flats inside again if the temperature took a sudden drop, so we cover the Quonset huts with plastic sheeting at night. We have on several occasions moved the seedlings to the terrace a little too early in the season and a heating device improvised for an emergency chill one year is now a standard piece of equipment. My hand hairdrier was attached to a thermostat set to turn the drier on when the temperature inside the Quonset hut dropped to 45 degrees. I sat up all night that first time, feeling relieved each time the plastic sheeting billowed when the hairdrier circulated the warm air inside the tent.

Keep the plants well watered during this transitional stage. They tend to harden when water is withheld, and their growth can be severely checked. Try to transplant the peat pots to the ground on a cloudy or even rainy day. Plants in peat pots should not wilt because there should be no root disturbance, but if they do, give water and cover the plants with newspaper for a day or two.

TOMATOES

Our predilection for tomatoes has led us to try to grow them under fluorescent lights. We had a fine tomato garden one year in a corner of the plant factory—plants growing at floor level and almost reaching the ceiling, and fluorescent lamps on the walls and ceiling. It can be done if you are stubborn enough, but really, it is not worth the effort. One feels guilty eating a tomato that cost ten dollars.

We start the seeds for our summer outdoor tomato plants about February 15, under lights. As soon as the plants are big enough to transplant to peat pots, they are moved to the fluorescent lights in the cool greenhouse. The plants are potted in 4-inch standard pots, then moved to 8- or 10-inch standard pots, and are flowering heavily by May 15 when they are moved outside. We do not plant the tomatoes in the ground, but set the large pots in an open coldframe and pack salt hay around the pots. Tall stakes are driven into the ground beside the pots to support the plants. The confinement of the roots in the restricted area of a pot produces magnificent plants and fruit. However, the selection of the strain of tomatoes to be grown this way is very important. We have tried many varieties and have found that two greenhouse or forcing varieties, 'Tuckcross O.' and 'Michigan State', are the best. They do as well outdoors as they do in the greenhouse for which they were bred. We have ripe fruit five to six weeks earlier than when we grew the usual outdoor varieties, and we strip enough green fruit from the plants in late October and early November, setting it to ripen in a cool dark place, to give us fresh tomatoes well into December.

HARDY BULBS

The spring flowering bulbs—those that will survive outdoors in cold climates—can be brought into flower easily with the aid of fluorescent light. Daffodils, hyacinths, tulips, crocus, chionodoxa, muscari, puschkinia, snowdrops, scilla, all of the hardy bulbs, need their outdoor cold treatment before forcing is attempted. The primary thing to bear in mind is that the bulbs must develop a good root system in cool or cold darkness before they are exposed to warmth and light. Bulb catalogs indicate which bulbs are early, intermediate and late flowering and usually also state the height of the plants at maturity. November 11 is my annual date for potting the hardy bulbs. The pots go into a coldframe in three layers, the latest flowering varieties on the bottom layer and the earliest ones on the top. Each bulb pan is covered with an inverted pot of the same size, salt hay is packed around the pots and the coldframe is covered with glass topped with burlap. The soil in the pots is thoroughly wet when the bulbs go into the coldframe and I have never had to give more water, although I do check them several times in November and December; all is lost if the soil dries. When sprouts are visible and roots appear through the drainage holes in the pots—late December for some—the plants are brought inside to a 50-degree temperature and kept in total darkness until the sprouts are about 3 inches high—two to three weeks. Then they are placed 10 to 12 inches below Gro-Lux lamps to bring on the flowers, still in the 50-degree temperature. They can be handled under lights in a warmer room, but forcing at the higher temperature is debilitating to the plant and the flowers last but a short time.

The old-fashioned refrigerator that lost status during a

kitchen remodeling project is in the garage. It is filled with pots of hardy bulbs on November 11, the thermostat set to hold the temperature at about 38°, and some of my best plants are produced by getting their cold treatment in the refrigerator. Also, I wrap a couple of pots of crocus in aluminum foil and put them in the household refrigerator. I am sure the reason this does not work as well as it might is that somebody looking for a midnight snack keeps unwrapping the packages. Following are some of the hardy bulbs that I plant in pots every year:

HYACINTH. *Very early* (can be in flower by Christmas): Jan Bos, L'Innocence. *Early:* Anne Marie, Arentine Arendsen, Bismarck, Cyclop, Edelweiss, Lord Balfour, Moreno, Nobel, Ostara, Perle Brilliant, Pink Pearl, Prince Henry, Van Tubergen's Scarlet. *February/March flowering:* Blue Danube, Blue Horizon, Carnegie, Delft Blue, Dr. Stresemann, Duke of Westminster, Gertrude, Grand Maitre, Jac Van Der Velde, Lady Derby, Marie, Myosotic, Orange Boven, Queen of the Whites, Sir William Mansfield, Yellow Hammer. *Late flowering:* Daylight, King of the Blues, King of the Lilacs, Marconi, Nankeen, Queen of the Blues, Queen of the Pinks, Queen of the Violets.

TULIPS. *Very early* (sometimes by Christmas): Brilliant Star, Duc van Thol cochineal, Duc van Thol scarlet, Duc van Thol white maxima. *Early* (January): Fuga, Louis Dupuy, Peach Blossom (has a lovely scent under the lights), Sonja. *February/ March:* Alberio, American Flag, De Wet, Fred Moore, Glory of Noordivijk, Golden Mascot, Haraut, King of the Yellows, Korneforos, Lady Moore, Nansen, Queen of the Night, Triumphator, Van der Eerden. *Late:* Queen of Bartigons.

NARCISSUS. The miniature species daffodils: *cyclamineus, Bulbocodium* var. *citrinum* (hoop), *Bulbocodium* var. *tenuifolius, canaliculatus, lobularis, minimus, scaberulus, triandrus albus* (angel's tears). Also Burgomaster Gouverneur, Cragford,

February Gold, Mrs. R. O. Backhouse, Peeping Tom, Queen of Bicolors, Rex, Silver Chimes, W. P. Milner.

HALF-HARDY BULBS

The half- or semi-hardy bulbs cannot stand freezing but they must be grown in a cool temperature. They can be potted and placed in a coldframe or trench, just as the hardy bulbs are, but they must come into a 45- or 50-degree temperature before there is any chance of their freezing. When rootlets show through the drainage holes in the pots, the procedure is the same as for the hardy bulbs.

My annual order to a bulb specialist includes one or two dozen each of several kinds of half-hardy bulbs belonging to two families. *Iridaceae* (iris family): babiana; freesia, gladiolus (I buy a potpourri called Herald Strain Rainbow Mix, and two white varieties, 'Colvillei The Bride' and 'Nanus Nymph'); bulbous iris, including the species *reticulata* which has a scent like violets, and the varieties 'Imperator' and 'Wedgewood'. In the *Liliaceae* (lily family) I always get *Sprekelia formosissima* (called Aztec lily, Jacobean lily, St. James lily)—I get two and sometimes three rounds of its spidery red flowers. Other half-hardy bulbs are the French Roman hyacinths; and *Narcissus Tazetta* (polyanthus narcissus), *N. Tazetta* var. *papyraceus* (paper-white narcissus), and *N. Tazetta* var. *orientalis* (Chinese sacred-lily).

The tender bulbs which must be handled as house plants the year around are listed by name in the alphabetical list of plants.

APPENDIX

Finding Lists

Knowledge is of two kinds: we know a subject ourselves,
or we know where we can find information upon it.

SAMUEL JOHNSON

Where to Buy House Plants, Supplies, and Fluorescent Light Equipment

It is exasperating to read or hear about beautiful house plants, to be told that you can grow them in your fluorescent light garden, and then to discover that you do not know where to get either plants or equipment. A mail-order supplier is often the best source. I have not personally purchased something from every supplier in the following list, but all of them have assured me in writing that they will be happy to serve the readers of this book. The list does not pretend to be complete so omission of a firm's name does not imply unreliability. It is wise to send for catalogs before ordering anything described in this book. Prices and specifications change, and you may find an item even better suited to your requirements than those I have mentioned.

I personally know a number of nurserymen who supply plants to amateur indoor gardeners. I have learned that some nurserymen growers are hobbyists who have "gone commercial." They serve us more from a love of the plants and a desire to help indoor gardeners to acquire rare and beautiful plants than they do because there is much profit in such a business. Catalogs are expensive to produce and some suppliers request a nominal fee for their catalogs. Most horticultural catalogs contain so much helpful information that I am glad to pay a small fee for them.

When requesting a catalog, print your name and full address and enclose the required coins, and mention that you got the supplier's name from this book. It is a courtesy practiced by amateur indoor gardeners to send a stamp when catalogs and lists are offered free.

ACKERMAN NURSERIES, Bridgman, Mich. 49106. House plants; catalog free.

ACME LITE PRODUCTS CO., INC., Congers, N. Y. 10920. Fluorescent light equipment; folder free.

ALBERTS & MERKEL BROS., INC., Box 537, Boynton Beach, Florida 33435. Orchids, bromeliads, gesneriads; catalog 25c.

ARTHUR EAMES ALLGROVE, N. Wilmington, Mass. 01888. Terrarium plants and supplies; catalog 25c.

ANTONELLI BROS., 2545 Capitola Road, Santa Cruz, Calif. 95062. Begonias, fuchsias, gloxinias, gesneriads; catalog 25c.

ARMSTRONG ASSOCIATES, INC., Box 127BK, Basking Ridge, N. J. 07920. Carnivorous plants, fluorescent light equipment; catalog 25c.

ARNDT'S FLORAL GARDEN, Rt. 2, Box 336, Troutdale, Ore. 97060. Gesneriads, begonias, house plants; catalog for 5c stamp.

BEAHM GARDENS, 2686 Paloma St., Pasadena, Calif. 91107. Epiphyllums, haworthias, hoyas; catalog free.

DOROTHY BIDDLE SERVICE, Hawthorne, N. Y. 10532. Arrangement supplies and material; catalog free.

BOYCAN'S FLORAL ARTS, State & Flowers Ave., Sharon, Pa. 16146. Arrangement supplies, cholla wood; catalog 25c.

BRECK'S OF BOSTON, 401 Summer St., Boston, Mass. 02210. Seeds, bulbs, supplies, fluorescent light equipment; catalog free.

BUELL'S GREENHOUSES, Eastford, Conn. 06242. Gloxinias, African violets, supplies, fluorescent light equipment; catalog 10c.

BURGESS SEED & PLANT CO., 67 E. Battle Creek St., Galesburg, Mich. 49053. House plants, supplies, fluorescent light equipment; catalog free.

W. ATLEE BURPEE CO., Phila., Pa. 19132, Clinton, Iowa 52733, Riverside, Calif. 92502. Seeds, house plants, fluorescent light equipment; catalog free.

BUYNAK'S, 3871 West 133rd, Cleveland 11, Ohio. African violets, other gesneriads; catalog 10c.

CALIFORNIA JUNGLE GARDENS, 11977 San Vicente Blvd., Los Angeles, Calif. 90049. Tropical plants; list free.

CENTRAL NURSERY CO., 2675 Johnson Ave., San Luis Obispo, Calif. 93401. Tropical plants and seeds; list 25c.

COOK'S GERANIUM NURSERY, 712 N. Grand, Lyons, Kansas. Geraniums; catalog 25c.

C. A. CRUICKSHANK, LTD., The Garden Guild, 1015 Mount Pleasant Road, Toronto 12, Ontario. Seeds, bulbs, plants, fluorescent light equipment *to Canadian points only;* catalog free.

P. DE JAGER & SONS, INC., 188 Asbury St., S. Hamilton, Mass. 01982. Hardy bulbs; catalog free.

DOROTHY J. DOLBOW, 149 W. Main St., Penns Grove, N. J. 08069. Sprays, insecticides, supplies; catalog free.

L. EASTERBROOK GREENHOUSES, 10 Craig St., Butler, Ohio 44822. African violets, gesneriads, supplies; list 15c.

EVERGLADES ENTERPRISES, P.O. Box 191, Tamiami Station, Miami, Florida 33144. Orchids, bromeliads, tropical plants; catalog 25c.

EVERGREEN HOUSE, 460 Scott Valley Drive, Santa Cruz, Calif. 95062. Bonsai plants and supplies; folder free for 4c stamp.

FARMER SEED & NURSERY CO., Faribault, Minn. 55021. House plants, fluorescent light equipment; catalog free.

FENNELL ORCHID CO., 26715 S. W. 157 Ave., Homestead, Florida. Orchids, supplies, fluorescent light equipment; catalog and "Orchid News" free.

FISCHER GREENHOUSES, Linwood, N. J. 08221. African violets, gesneriads, supplies; catalog 10c.

FLORALITE CO., 4124 E. Oakwood Road, Oak Creek, Wis. Fluorescent light equipment; folder free.

FOGG-IT NOZZLE CO., P. O. Box 11127, Oakland, Calif. 94611. Fine-spray nozzles; catalog sheet free.

J. HOWARD FRENCH, 1215 W. Baltimore Pike, Lima, Pa. 19060. Seeds, bulbs, supplies; catalog free.

JAMES I. GEORGE & SON, INC., Fairport, N. Y. 14450. Clematis; catalog free.

GERRY'S GERANIUM GARDEN, P. O. Box 1355, Artesia, Calif. Geraniums; catalog 10c.

GIRARD NURSERIES, Geneva, Ohio 44041. Azaleas, bonsai; catalog free.

ROBERT D. GOEDERT, Box 6534, Jacksonville, Florida 32205. Amaryllis bulbs; catalog free.

GRANGER GARDENS, R. 2, Box 289, Medina, Ohio. African violets, gesneriads; list 10c.

BERNARD D. GREESON, 3548 N. Cramer St., Milwaukee, Wis. 53211. Fluorescent light equipment, supplies in small quantities; list 10c.

GROWERS SUPPLY CO., P. O. Box 1132, Ann Arbor, Mich. 48103. Fluorescent light equipment; folders free.

LUE HALE, BLUE WHALE GARDENS, Box 413, Lake Oswego, Ore. 97034. Fertilizers, rare seeds; list free.

HARROLD'S PANSY GARDENS & GREENHOUSES, P. O. Box 29, Grants Pass, Ore. 97526. Begonias, gesneriads, other house plants; seeds; catalog 10c.

JOSEPH HARRIS CO., INC., Moreton Farm, Rochester, N. Y. 14624. Seeds, supplies; catalog free.

HILLTOP FARM, R. 3, Box 216, Cleveland, Texas 77327. Herbs, scented geraniums; list 20c.

HOUDYSHEL'S NURSERY, 1412 Third St., LaVerne, Calif. African violets, bromeliads, fluorescent light equipment; list free.

THE HOUSE PLANT CORNER, Box 810, Oxford, Md. 21654. Supplies, equipment, fluorescent light equipment; catalog 20c.

HYDROPONIC CHEMICAL CO., INC., Box 97-C, Copley, Ohio 44321. Hyponex plant foods, insecticides, Wik-Fed pots; catalog free.

MARGARET ILGENFRITZ, Box 665, Monroe, Mich. 48161. Orchids; catalog 50c.

JACK'S CACTUS GARDEN, 1707 W. Robindale St., W. Covina, California 91790. Cacti, succulents, cholla log pots, seeds; list 10c.

JOHNSON CACTUS GARDENS, Box 458, Paramount, Calif. 90724. Cacti, succulents, supplies; catalog 10c.

KARTUZ GREENHOUSES, 92 Chestnut St., Wilmington, Mass. 01887. Begonias, African violets, gesneriads, supplies; A.V. list free; catalog indicating plants for fluorescent light culture, 25c.

MRS. A. W. KNOCK, 5833 Second Ave. S., Minneapolis, Minn. 55419. Seeds of gesneriads and begonias; list free for stamped addressed envelope.

LAGER & HURRELL, 426 Morris Ave., Summit, N. J. 07901. Orchids, supplies; List HG describing orchids suited to fluorescent light culture free.

LOGEE'S GREENHOUSES, 55 North St., Danielson, Conn. 06239. Begonias, geraniums, tropicals; catalog 25c.

LYNDON LYON, 14 Mutchler St., Dolgeville, N. Y. 13329. Plants and cuttings of African violets and columneas; list free.

MAYFAIR NURSERIES, R. D. 2, Nichols, N. Y. 13812. Dwarf plants; list free.

ROD MC LELLAN CO., 1450 El Camino Real, S. San Francisco, Calif. 94080. Orchids, supplies; catalog free.

MERRY GARDENS, Camden, Maine 04843. Tropical plants; lists free, catalog 25c.

JOHN MESSELAAR BULB CO., INC., P. O. Box 269, County Road, Ipswich, Mass. 01938. Flower bulbs; list free.

HOLMES C. MILLER, 280 W. Portola Ave., Los Altos, Calif. 94022. Zonal geraniums including dwarfs; catalog 10c.

SHIRLEY MORGAN, Mail Box Seeds, 2042 Encinal Ave., Alameda, Calif. 94501. Seeds of herbs, indoor plants; list 30c.

WALTER F. NICKE, Box 71, Hudson, N. Y. 12534. Labels, pocket pruner, sprayers; "Garden Talk" free.

NIES NURSERY, 5710 S. W. 37th St., W. Hollywood, Florida 33020. Palms, tropical house plants; catalog free.

NORVELL GREENHOUSES, 318 S. Greenacres Road, Greenacres, Wash. 99016. African violets, cacti, odd and rare house plants; catalog free.

OAKHURST GARDENS, P. O. Box 444, Arcadia, Calif. 91008. Unusual bulbs, bromeliads, miniature and botanical orchids; catalog 35c.

L. L. OLDS SEED COMPANY, 722 Williamson St., Madison, Wis. 53701. House plant bulbs, supplies, fluorescent light equipment; catalog free.

GEO. W. PARK SEED CO., Box 31, Greenwood, S. Carolina 29647. Seeds, plants, bulbs, supplies, fluorescent light equipment; catalog free.

PEARCE SEED CO., Moorestown, N. J. House plants, seeds; list free.

PENNSYLVANIA STATE UNIVERSITY CORRESPONDENCE COURSES, 202 Agricultural Education Bldg., University Park, Pa. 16802. Correspondence courses in indoor gardening; catalog free.

PETER PAULS NURSERIES, R.D. 4, Canadaigua, N. Y. 14424. Seeds, cacti, bonsai, terrarium plants, ferns, fluorescent light equipment; catalog free.

J. A. PETERSON SONS, 3132 McHenry Ave., Cincinnati, Ohio 45211. African violets, gesneriads; minimum order 25 plants by express; list free.

PLANT GROWTH SUPPLIES, P. O. Box 8543-A, Greenville, S. Carolina 29604. Fluorescent light equipment; folders free for 5c stamp.

PLANT MARVEL LABORATORIES, 624 W. 119th St., Chicago 28, Ill. 60628. Water-soluble plant foods, aerosol insecticides; supplies; list free.

PLANTSMITH, P. O. Box 818, Palo Alto, Calif. Spoonit plant foods; sample free on request.

POULETTE PRODUCTS, Kempton, Pa. 19529. Garden-Gate swinging plant racks; leaflet free.

PRIPLATA FOUNTAINS, 408 N. Fair Oaks Ave., Pasadena, Calif. 91103. Indoor water fountains complete or parts; fluorescent light equipment; catalog 50c.

RANSOM SEED CO., Box 1096, Arcadia, Calif. 91006. Seeds, hotbed kits; catalog 10c.

HARVEY J. RIDGE, 1126 Arthur Street, Wausau, Wis. 54401. Supplies, equipment, plastic markers, fluorescent light equipment; list free.

ROAD RUNNER RANCH, 2458 Catalina Ave., Vista, Calif. 92083. Geraniums for collectors, herbs; catalog free.

MRS. ROSE MAILORDERS, Box 11206, Philadelphia, Pa. 19117. Miniature greenhouse, planting trays, supplies; circulars free.

HARRY E. SAIER, Dimondale, Mich. 48821. Seeds; catalog 50c.

MAX SCHLING, SEEDSMEN, INC., 538 Madison Ave., New York, N. Y. 10022. House plants, supplies, fluorescent light equipment; catalogs free.

SELECT VIOLET HOUSE, Box 1444, Youngstown, Ohio 44501. African violets, gesneriads, fluorescent light equipment; list free for stamped addressed envelope.

SEQUOIA NURSERY, 2519 E. Mineral King, Visalia, Calif. 93277. Miniature bush, tree and climbing roses; folder free.

SHOPLITE CO., 650 Franklin Ave., Nutley, N. J. 07110. Fluorescent light equipment, accessories, kits, parts; catalog 10c.

MRS. JOHN SLIVKA, 203 N. Ohio St., Fayette, Ohio 43521. African violets, gesneriads, supplies; list free for 5c stamp.

SOUTH SHORE FLORAL CO., 1050 Quentin Place, Woodmere, N. Y. 11598. Arrangement supplies and equipment; catalog free.

SPIDELL'S FINE PLANTS, 1380 Garfield St., Eugene, Ore. 97402. African violets, gesneriads, supplies, fluorescent light equipment; catalog free.

SPONGE-ROK HORTICULTURAL PERLITE, P. O. Box 83, Paramount,

Calif. 90723. Horticultural perlite in four grades; list, literature free.

FRED A. STEWART, INC., P. O. Box 307, San Gabriel, Calif. 91775. Orchids, supplies; catalog free.

TERRACE VIEW GARDENS, Indianapolis Road, Greencastle, Ind. Peperomias, ivies, unusual house plants; list free for 5c stamp.

THREE SPRINGS FISHERIES, Lilypons, Maryland 21717. Miniature water lily for indoor aquariums; aquatic plants; fluorescent light equipment; catalog free.

TINARI GREENHOUSES, 2325 Valley Road, Bethayres, Pa. 19006 African violets, gesneriads, supplies, fluorescent light equipment, catalog free.

TINY TREES NURSERY CO., 5212 N. Peck Road, El Monte, Calif. 91731. Bonsai and supplies; catalog 10c.

TROPICAL GARDENS, RR 1, Box 143, Greenwood, Indiana. Gesneriads; list free for 5c stamp.

TROPICAL PARADISE GREENHOUSES, 8825 W. 79th, Overland Park, Kansas 66200. House plants, supplies; catalog 50c.

TUBE CRAFT, INC., 1311 W. 80th St., Cleveland, Ohio 44102. FloraCart, fiberglass trays, timers, watering aid; catalog free.

UNION PRODUCTS, INC., 511 Lancaster St., Leominster, Mass. 01453. Plastic pots, pot racks, miniature greenhouses, accessories; catalog free.

VAN NESS WATER GARDENS, 2460 N. Euclid Ave., Upland, Calif. 91786. Water lilies, aquatics, supplies; catalog free.

VAN SCIVER'S DUTCH GARDENS, Pocono Mts., Box 12, Tannersville, Pa. 18372. Begonia tubers, Dutch bulbs; list free.

VETTERLE & REINELT, P. O. Box 125, Capitola, Calif. 95010. Tuberous begonias, supplies; catalog free.

VI'S SELECT SEED SHOP, 307 So. Maple St., Watertown, S. Dakota 57201. Seed, planting kits, "Water 'N Watch" pre-seeded indoor gardens; list free for stamped addressed envelope.

VOLKMANN BROS. GREENHOUSES, 2714 Minert St., Dallas, Texas 75219. African violets and supplies; list free.

THE WALKERS, Box 150, 906 S. Pecan St., Luling, Texas 78648. Supplies, fluorescent light equipment; list free for 4c stamp.

JEAN WEST, 201 Penn N.W., Warren, Ohio 44480. Rare house plant seeds; list free for stamped addressed envelope.

WHISTLING HILL, Maude C. Cogswell, P. O. Box 27, Hamburg, N. Y. 14075. Gesneriads only; list 10c.

MRS. N. B. WILSON, 41 Love St., Austell, Georgia 30001. African violets, begonias, pots; list free for 5c stamp.

WILSON BROS., Roachdale, Indiana 46172. Geraniums, house plants; catalog free.

WILSONS TROPICAL GARDENS & PLANT OF THE MONTH CLUB, Box 45, Ganges, British Columbia. Gesneriads, plant-of-month club; lists free to all but plants shipped only to Canadian points.

YOHO & HOOKER, 523 Williamson Ave., Youngstown, Ohio 44501. Supplies, equipment, fluorescent light equipment; lists free.

Helpful Periodicals for Indoor Gardeners

African Violet Magazine, quarterly, African Violet Society of America, P. O. Box 1326, Knoxville, Tennessee 37901.

American Camellia Journal and Yearbook, American Camellia Society, Joseph H. Pyron, P. O. Box C, Tifton, Georgia.

American Fern Journal, American Fern Society, Mrs. Geoffroy Atkinson, 415 S. Pleasant Street, Amherst, Massachusetts 01002.

American Orchid Society Bulletin, monthly, American Orchid Society, Botanical Museum of Harvard University, Cambridge, Mass. 02138.

The Begonian, monthly, American Begonia Society, Mrs. Daisy Austin, 1510 Kimberly Avenue, Anaheim, California 92802.

Bromeliad Society Bulletin, bimonthly, The Bromeliad Society, Jeanne Woodbury, 1811 Edgecliffe Drive, Los Angeles 26, California.

Bulletin, annual, American Poinsettia Society, Mrs. R. E. Gaunt, Box 94, Mission, Texas 78572.

Bulletin, bimonthly, Epiphyllum Society of America, Gene Luckenbacher, 4400 Portola Avenue, Los Angeles 32, California.

Cactus and Succulent Journal, bimonthly, 132 W. Union Street, Pasadena, California.

Geraniums Around the World, quarterly, International Geranium Society, Mrs. Vernon Ireland, 1413 Bluff Drive, Santa Barbara, California.

Gesneriad-Saintpaulia News (GSN), bimonthly, Saintpaulia International, Alma Wright, P. O. Box 10604, Knoxville, Tennessee 37919.

The Gloxinian and the Other Gesneriads, bimonthly, American Gloxinia Society, Mrs. Diantha Buell, Eastford, Connecticut 06242.

National Chrysanthemum Society Bulletin, bimonthly, Miss Dorothy P. Tuthill, 345 Milton Road, Rye, New York.

The National Fuchsia Fan, monthly, California National Fuchsia Society, Mrs. Maxine Butler, 6124 So. Rimbank Avenue, Pico Rivera, California, 90661.

Orchidata, monthly, Greater New York Orchid Society, Mrs. Thomas Powell, 338 East 83rd Street, New York 28, New York.

Plant Life, quarterly, American Plant Life Society, Thomas W. Whitaker, Box 150, La Jolla, California.

The Seed Pod, quarterly, American Hibiscus Society, James E. Monroe, P. O. Box 98, Eagle Lake, Florida.

Books

Like most amateur gardeners, I read horticultural books incessantly. Sometimes I garden with a book in one hand and a plant in the other, until I learn the ways of a plant new to my garden. Listed are some of the books in my horticultural library—books whose pages are dog-eared and marked with my own marginal notations. There are many other horticultural books beside these, and the omission of a title does not imply that it is not a good book. If I, as an amateur gardener, were limited to two books, I would unhesitatingly select *Hortus Second* and a good dictionary. As a garden writer, to those two I would add the booklet, *International Code of Nomenclature for Cultivated Plants 1961*.

An asterisk preceding a title indicates that the book is of a technical nature.

AFRICAN VIOLETS, GLOXINIAS AND THEIR RELATIVES, A Guide to the Cultivated Gesneriads, Harold E. Moore, Jr. New York, Macmillan, 1957.

ALL ABOUT BEGONIAS, Bernice Brilmayer. New York, Doubleday, 1960.

ALL ABOUT MINIATURE PLANTS AND GARDENS, Bernice Brilmayer. New York, Doubleday, 1963.

ALL ABOUT VINES AND HANGING PLANTS, Bernice Brilmayer. New York, Doubleday, 1962.

AMARYLLIS AND HOW TO GROW THEM, Peggie Schulz. New York, Barrows, 1954.

THE ART OF TRAINING PLANTS, Ernesta Drinker Ballard. New York, Harper, 1962.

BONSAI: MINIATURE TREES, Claude Chidamian. Princeton, N. J., Van Nostrand, 1955.

A BOOK ABOUT SOILS FOR THE HOME GARDENER, H. Stuart Ortloff and · Henry B. Raymore. New York, Barrows, 1962.

THE BOOK OF CACTI AND OTHER SUCCULENTS, Claude Chidamian. New York, Doubleday, 1958.

BOTANY FOR GARDENERS, Harold William Rickett. New York, Macmillan, 1957.

BULB MAGIC IN YOUR WINDOW, Ruth Marie Peters. New York, Barrows, 1954.

CACTI FOR THE AMATEUR, Scott E. Haselton. Pasadena, Calif., Abbey Garden Press, 1958.

CACTUS GUIDE, Ladislaus Cutak. Princeton, N. J., Van Nostrand, 1956.

*COMMERCIAL FLOWER FORCING, Alex Laurie, D. C. Kiplinger, Kennard S. Nelson. New York, McGraw-Hill, 1958.

THE COMPLETE BOOK OF GREENHOUSE GARDENING, Henry T. and Rebecca T. Northen. New York, Ronald, 1956.

DAFFODILS, OUTDOORS AND IN, Carey E. Quinn. New York, Hearthside, 1959.

DISEASES AND PESTS OF ORNAMENTAL PLANTS, P. P. Pirone, Bernard O. Dodds, Harold W. Rickett. New York, Ronald, 1960.

*FLORICULTURE, Alex Laurie and Victor H. Ries. New York, McGraw-Hill, 1950.

GARDEN IN YOUR HOUSE, Ernesta Drinker Ballard. New York, Harper, 1958.

GARDEN POOLS, WATER LILIES, AND GOLDFISH, G. L. Thomas, Jr. Princeton, N. J., Van Nostrand, 1958.

THE GARDENER'S FERN BOOK, Gordon Foster. Princeton, N. J., Van Nostrand, 1964.

GARDENING IN A SMALL GREENHOUSE, Mary Noble and J. L. Merkle. Princeton, N. J., Van Nostrand, 1956.

GLOXINIAS AND HOW TO GROW THEM, Peggie Schulz. New York, Barrows, 1953.

GROWING ORCHIDS AT YOUR WINDOWS, Jack Kramer. Princeton, N. J., Van Nostrand, 1963.

GROWTH OF PLANTS, William Crocker. New York, Reinhold, 1948.

HOME ORCHID GROWING, Rebecca T. Northen. Princeton, N. J., Van Nostrand, 1950.

HORTUS SECOND, A Concise Dictionary of Gardening and General Horticulture, L. H. Bailey and Ethel Zoe Bailey. New York, Macmillan, 1941.

HOW TO CONTROL PLANT DISEASES, Malcolm Shurtleff. Ames, Iowa, Iowa State University Press, 1963.

HOW TO GROW RARE GREENHOUSE PLANTS, Ernest Chabot. New York, Barrows, 1952.

HOW TO MAKE MONEY FROM YOUR HOME GREENHOUSE, Peggie Schulz. Princeton, N. J., Van Nostrand, 1959.

INTERNATIONAL CODE OF NOMENCLATURE FOR CULTIVATED PLANTS, 1961. Utrecht, Netherlands, International Bureau for Plant Taxonomy and Nomenclature of the International Association for Plant Taxonomy, 1961. Obtainable from American Hosticultural Society, 1600 Bladensburg Road, N.E., Washington, D.C. 20002, for fifty cents.

THE JOY OF GERANIUMS, Helen Van Pelt Wilson. New York, Barrows, 1965.

*LIGHT AND PLANT GROWTH, R. Van Der Veen and G. Meijer. Eindhoven, Holland, Philips' Technical Library, 1959. Distributed by Macmillan, New York.

*LIGHT, PHOTOMETRY AND ILLUMINATING ENGINEERING, William E. Barrows. New York, McGraw-Hill, 1938. (Out of print)

MINIATURE GARDENS, Anne Ashberry. Princeton, N. J., Van Nostrand, 1952.

MINIATURE PLANTS FOR HOME AND GREENHOUSE, Elvin McDonald. Princeton, N. J., Van Nostrand, 1962.

THE MINIATURE ROSE BOOK, Margaret E. Pinney. Princeton, N. J., Van Nostrand, 1964.

THE NEW COMPLETE BOOK OF AFRICAN VIOLETS, Helen Van Pelt Wilson. New York, Barrows, 1963.

THE NEW GREENHOUSE GARDENING FOR EVERYONE, Ernest Chabot. New York, Barrows, 1955.

1001 HOUSE PLANT QUESTIONS ANSWERED, Stanley Schuler. Princeton, N. J., Van Nostrand, 1963.

ORCHIDS AS HOUSE PLANTS, Rebecca T. Northen. Princeton, N. J., Van Nostrand, 1955.

PLANT DISEASE HANDBOOK, Cynthia Westcott. Princeton, N. J., Van Nostrand, 1960.

PLANT PROPAGATION IN PICTURES, Montague Free. New York, Doubleday, 1957.

PLANTS INDOORS, Mary Noble and J. L. Merkel. Princeton, N. J., Van Nostrand, 1954.

PRACTICAL PLANT BREEDING, W. J. C. Lawrence. London, George Allen & Unwin, Ltd., 1948.

*PROPAGATION OF HORTICULTURAL PLANTS, Guy W. Adriance and Fred R. Brison, New York, McGraw-Hill, 1955.

THE SECRET OF THE GREEN THUMB, Henry T. and Rebecca T. Northen. New York, Ronald, 1954.

SUCCULENTS FOR THE AMATEUR, arranged and edited by Scott E. Haselton. Pasadena, Calif., Abbey Garden Press, 1955.

TUBEROUS BEGONIAS, Worth Brown. New York, Barrows, 1955.

THE WONDERFUL WORLD OF BULBS, Bebe Miles. Princeton, N. J., Van Nostrand, 1963.

THE WORLD BOOK OF HOUSE PLANTS, Elvin McDonald. New York, World, 1963.

1201 AFRICAN VIOLET QUESTIONS ANSWERED BY TWENTY EXPERTS, Helen Van Pelt Wilson. Princeton, N. J., Van Nostrand, 1965.

YOUR GARDEN SOIL, R. Milton Carleton. Princeton, N. J., Van Nostrand, 1961.

Also these pamphlets and booklets published at irregular intervals:

AGRICULTURAL RESEARCH SERVICE, USDA, Beltsville, Maryland. Bulletins on light and plant growth.

BROOKLYN BOTANIC GARDEN, Brooklyn, New York 11225. Handbooks on many horticultural subjects.

SYLVANIA ELECTRIC PRODUCTS, INC., Commercial Engineering Dept., Salem, Mass. Gro-Lux Fluorescent Lamp bulletins, free.

Index

Onagraceae, 185
Oncidium cheirophorum, 202
1-1-1 potting mix, 101
Opuntia, 166
orange, 171
orange Browallia, 218
Orchidaceae, 199
Orchids, 199-203
organic soil, 96
organ pipe Cactus, 166
Oriental bellflower, 196
ornamental cotton, 187
Ornithocephalus bicornis, 202
Osmanthus fragrans, 203
outdoor garden, 221
Oxalidaceae, 203
Oxalis hedysaroides rubra, 203
oxygen, 92, 115, 116
oyster shells, 22, 115

paint, flat white, 53
Palmaceae, 173
panda plant, 194
pan fixture; see strip fixture
paper-white Narcissus, 227
Parodia aureispina, 166
patient plant, 192
peacock foliage plant, 180
Peat-Lite potting mixes, 100
peat moss, 22. See also potting media
peat pots, 222
Pelargonium, 204-206
    fancy-leaved, 5, 204, 205
    ivy-leaved, 29, 204
Pellionia, 206
Peperomia, 4, 206
perforated fixture, 55
perlite, 22
pests, 26, 122
pH, 104-105
Philodendron, 32
phosphorus, 109
photoelectric switch, 130-131
photographic exposure meter, 79
photonasty, 63
photoperiodism, 62, 73
photoreactions of plants, 61-65, 73
photosynthesis, 59, 62, 92

phototaxis, 63
phototropism, 63
phytochrome, 63
phytoillumination, v
piggy-back plant, 219
Pilea, 207
pincushion Cactus, 166
Piperaceae, 206
Plant-Gro lamps, 68, 69
plant growth lamps, 68-70
plant nutrition; see fertilizers
plasterer's lath, 28
plastic
    for lining benches, 22
    miniature greenhouses, 127
    pot racks, 31
    pots, 107
    sheeting, 90
platforms for plants, 26
Pleispilos, 207
poinsettia, 181
polyanthus Narcissus, 227
Polystichum tsus-simense, 183
pomegranate, 208
ponderosa lemon, 170
potash; see potassium
potassium, 109, 110
pot hooks, 31
pot racks, 31
pots, 107, 108
potting media, 96-105, 150. See also 143-228
potting plants, 106
pouch flower, 192
Poulette Welding Co., 31
powder puff Cactus, 166
Powell, Thomas, x, 200
powergroove lamp, 42
powertube lamp, 42
powertwist lamp, 42
prayer plant, 197
preheat fixture, 38
preheat lamp, 40
Prescott, Mrs. William, vi, x, 7, 8, 23, 30, 184
prickly pear Cactus, 166
propagation, 27, 69, 124-129, 151. See also 143-228